Donald L Johnson
October 2018

Dedication

This book is dedicated to those many sailors who went to sea in those small and fragile, yet workhorse greyhounds of the sea, the "tin cans" and especially to those who gave all and remain at watch on the high seas.

The book is a compilation of images and first-person accounts, providing a glimpse of what it was like living at sea, often in hostile environments — both natural for manmade — and for extended periods of time.

The book is a glimpse into the past - a look at the present - and a taste of the future.

The book serves a variety of readers:

- If you served on these ships especially in time of war - to give you a renewed sense of patriotic contribution to a nation you love.
- If you are family of those sailors ... a mother or father left behind..
- A grandmother or grandfather left behind ... a wife left behind.
- A son or daughter or a grandchild who wonders ... *"what did dad or grandpa do during the war? what was it like?"*
- A brother or sister left behind.
- A good friend left behind
- If you are today's sailor seeking a legacy for your service.
- If you are just the naturally curious type... curious about tough and monumental times in history - times that changed the course of history.

Some went down to the sea in ships, doing business on the great waters; they saw the great deeds of the Lord, His wondrous works in the deep. For He commanded and raised the stormy wind, which lifted up the waves of the sea.

©2018 by Don Johnson who retains sole copyright to his contributions to this book.

I thank you for looking at this book. If you have enjoyed it and wish to purchase copies, visit:
amazon.com/author/donjohnsonbooks

Or contact me at:
DonJohnsonDD682@live.com

About the cover photo:

They left on ships – they left on planes – they left on trains. All must be remembered … those that left
and those that were left behind to wait.

As you read this book, look at a 20-minute companion video. It will give you a real-world appreciation of the pictorial images and narrative in the book.

http://www.youtube.com/watch?v=sloZqBsalZc

Contents

Dedication ii
The evolution of the US Navy Destroyer 3
The evolution of the US Navy sailor 5
The mighty and majestic sea 12
The Secret of the Sea 16
Man Overboard & Rescue at Sea 18
Man Overboard: The rest of the story 22
A Navy community at sea 26
Plane Guard 34
Naval Gunfire support 38
US Navy: A Global Force for Good! 57
Valor at the Vietnam war's end: 71
The Hell of battle damage 87
Collisions: a constant concern 111
Sr. Chief Rob O'Neill -A hometown hero 131
Off Duty - Liberty Call 148
And what of those tin can sailors? 150
"Pivot Point" 163
Some Final Tributes 172
Recommended reading and browsing: 183
Museum Ships 185
HOW TO SIMULATE BEING A SAILOR 190
The places we lived 194
Heritage 199
About the author 200
Some reader remarks on this book 201

There was a little something Machinist's Made third class Jim Devin, a husky six-foot, 200-pound sailor from Chula Vista, California had to tell his wife, Janece, yesterday when Devin's ship came home from the Western Pacific. He told her while he and Mrs. Devin stood by a rail near where it happened last April 5, 60 miles off the coast of Southern Japan. "I fell overboard, " said Devin, 22. "You didn't!" said Mrs. Devin, her eyes widening. "Well, I did, " Devin said, "and I bobbed around in a big storm for two hours. " He hadn't written to her about the incident, Devin told his wife of seven months, because he wanted to tell her of his brush with death in person.

(More on Jim Devin later so be looking for it)

USS Roper (DD-147)
1918 Wickes class

USS Balch (DD-363)
1936 Porter class

USS Porterfield (DD-682)
1943 Fletcher class

USS Laffey (DD-724)
1944 Sumner class

USS Sellers (DDG-II)
1961 Adams class

USS Arleigh Burke (DDG-51)
1991 Burke class

The evolution of the US Navy Destroyer

There have been many classes of destroyers over the years, and here are just a few including the futuristic Zumwalt class still under construction and due in the fleet in 2015.

Perhaps the most iconic of the tin cans is the Fletcher class, of which 175 were commissioned between 1942 and 1944, more than any other class. I'll admit to a bias towards the Fletcher since I served on the USS Porterfield and also reserve duty on the USS Shields (DD-596).

The Fletcher design was generally regarded as highly successful. Fletchers had a design speed of 38 knots, armed with five 5" guns in single mounts and carrying 10 21" torpedoes in twin quintuple centerline mounts. The Allen M. Sumner and Gearing classes were Fletcher derivatives, thus Fletcher had a larger influence than the original design.

The evolution of the US Navy sailor

And as we saw the destroyers evolving from the old 4-stacker Roper to the futuristic Zumwalt, so young sailors must mature into efficient fighting machines. This begins in Boot Camp where precious things are left behind -- girlfriends, hair, a little bit of dignity and mom doing the laundry.

That forlorn look on the young sailor's face is saying: *"can't I just go home before you hang me on that rack like the rest of them?"* And yes, that is an armed sailor diligently guarding the laundry.

But before long we recruits - mere lads - matured into seasoned salts ready for the high seas and adventure.

My own sea story: Growing Up

This is one of those "growing up moments" we all hopefully go through. In boot camp I became one of the privileged few because I had a year of college. I and several others also having a bit of college, were made Recruit Petty Officers. These were cushy jobs and all we had to do was to lord it over those lesser guys that had no college. Well, of course, this skinny little kid put on a lot of weight, mostly in the head as it swelled and swelled with self-importance. After boot camp, I went to an A school where I learned a bit about my next job as a Fire Control Technician (FT).

When I reported aboard the USS Porterfield (DD-682) as the new kid and still with the big head, I was greeted warmly (yea) and immediately sent down to the mess deck where I spent the next many months preparing for and cleaning up after the meals. And no, I was not a cook.

The hours were long, beginning in the wee hours before breakfast and ending after cleanup of the evening meal. Gone were the cushy days of boot camp and school this was the real Navy, and I was low man.

One night I was swabbing the deck and anxious to get out of there. I was doing a half-assed job of it and I knew it more importantly the Master at Arms of the mess deck, a 2'nd class electrician named John Terrell knew it. If you remember Ken Norton, the guy that broke Mohammed Ali's jaw well Terrell was built a lot like Norton.

So Terrell and I went nose to nose, probably at least a half second or so, before I found myself down on the deck with only a bucket, a sponge and a scouring pad (no John did not knock me down). And I cleaned that entire deck corner to corner on my hands and knees.

In those hours and minutes of scouring that deck, my head somehow shrunk down to its former size and I learned a valuable lesson ... I understood my place and I understood who was boss ... and it wasn't me. I cherish that experience because it helped me to grow up. And I respected Terrell for doing what needed to be done and have never held any grudge towards him ... then or now.

And this from Chief Petty Officer Jaime Picoe
- on leadership -

... Somewhere along the line, when we weren't looking, it happened. We might not have noticed at first. People would stop talking and listen when you spoke up. People would come and seek your advice, your opinion. Newbies would wander over wanting just to be around you. Seniors would send junior enlisted to work for or with you. "Old Timers" wouldn't bat an eye when you came up and had a beer with them. Didn't really matter how or why you enlisted, you came in as "a Kid." And then "you" grew up. And when you went home, all those you left behind might tilt their head and half squint to look at you, and those words would come, "You've changed." It would stop you in your tracks, and give you pause to sink in. Oh, you might doubt and deny, question or be confused, for you don't feel any different, grown or lost any weight, but they see it in you. It does that you know. Like it or not. I remember reading a book that spoke of "the Rite of Passage. " In it a cabin boy, transferring from one whaler to another whaler, had to swim across from ship to ship, for they weren't going to waste time lowering a boat. You had to earn the right to sail aboard her. Didn't we all do the same? No matter if you did 2, 4, 6, or 20 years in. Somewhere you changed, and not just where the hair started to grow, and not just because that woman in the bar overseas took you home. You started to back up your own B.S. with knowledge and skills. You learned to deal with people who weren't related to you, nor cared who you were related to, or who you knew. Yeah, you may have looked stupid at times, yeah you made mistakes, but you learned from errors and did better next time. You grew up! And you had shipmates and a long line of Naval tradition that helped you to do so. And then it became your turn to help the "New Kid"! I did my turn, hope you did yours.

And again from the Chief - on Memorial Day-

On Memorial Day Weekend Sometime this weekend ... I will recall one of the first times I ever heard and "finally understood" the emotions that went along with "Taps" . It was almost dark with only the hint of light left in the western sky ... off in the distance, the muffled sounds of a barracks full of men ending their day ... the first notes broke and I remembered what was to come next, stopped and stood to listen ... as the tune continued on, I remember the soft press of "something" in my chest, a bit of something needing to be swallowed in my throat - images of blurred people standing about me ... a bit of loneliness and sorrow within ... and as the final notes sounded, the release of · the breath I had held in, and a tired droop of my shoulders ....the quiet and the dark deepened and surrounded me ... I felt a bit "old & tired" in need of rest and sleep. As I walked on, I remembered those almost forgotten, now passed on ... those looking toward the light and life, now standing in darkness ... I too have a place amongst them ... just not now ...   just   not   now.

"There is something singularly beautiful and appropriate in the music of this wonderful call. Its strains are melancholy, yet full of rest and peace. Its echoes linger in the heart long after its tones have ceased to vibrate in the air." — Oliver Wilcox Norton

The mighty and majestic sea

Life at sea is viewed and experienced differently by each sailor and is certainly colored by the events surrounding the experiences.

A war-time deployment is different than a peace-time deployment, and each war brings on unique circumstances ... my experience is the Vietnam War experience.

The WW-II deployment of the four sailors I met recently at a Porterfield reunion was a long 2 years - seven months and 24 days, campaigning against a very powerful Japanese Navy.

The Korean War deployment of the sailors I met at that same reunion was also long and arduous. One sailor talked of operating in minus 38-degree weather off the North Korean coast with no inside passageways providing shelter when going fore and aft.

What I will try to capture in the pages to follow is what was typical of my 1966 cruise to what is called WestPac (Western Pacific). Other years and other wars, though different, were probably somewhat similar. Mind you, when we set sail for WestPac that January of 1966, I don't recall knowing of a war going on over there, nor do I recall ever having heard of the country 'Vietnam."

Our typical evolution, as I recall, was a three-day affair:

- Plane Guarding aircraft carrier flight operations.
- Naval Gun Fire Support (NGFS) of Marines and soldiers on shore.
- Replenishment (fuel, ammo, food, mail, movies)

The seas were not always kind ... nor the winds calm at our backs

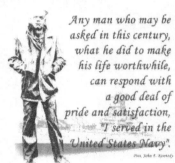

The Secret of the Sea
By Henry Wadsworth Longfellow

Ah! what pleasant visions haunt me
As I gaze upon the sea!
All the old romantic legends,
All my dreams, come back to me.

Sails of silk and ropes of sandal,
Such as gleam in ancient lore;
And the singing of the sailors,
And the answer from the Shore!

Most of all, the Spanish ballad
Haunts me oft, and tarries long,
Of the noble Count Arnaldos
And the sailor's mystic song.

Like the long waves on a sea-beach,
Where the sand as silver shines
With a soft, monotonous cadence,
Flow its unrhymed lyric lines:

Telling how the Count Arnaldos,
With his hawk upon his hand,
Saw a fair and stately galley.
Steering onward to the land;

How he heard the ancient helmsman
Chant a song so wild and clear,
That the sailing sea-bird slowly
Poised upon the mast to hear,

Till his soul was full of longing,
And he cried, With impulse strong,
"Helmsman! for the love of heavn,
Teach me too, that wondrous song!

Wouldst thou, "so the helmsman answered,
"Learn the secret of the sea?
Only those who brave its dangers
Comprehend its mystery!"

In each sail that skims the horizon,
In each landward-blowing breeze,
I behold that stately galley,
Hear those mournful melodies;

Till my soul is full of longing
For the secret of the sea,
And the heart of the great ocean
Sends a thrilling pulse through me.

"I waited. And then, true to His promise, He came into my heart and my life. The moment was more than remarkable; it was the most realistic experience I'd ever had. I'm not sure what I expected; perhaps my life or my sins or a great white light would flash before my eyes; perhaps I'd feel a shock like being hit by a bolt of lightning. Instead, I felt no tremendous sensation, just a weightlessness and an enveloping calm that let me know that Christ had come into my heart."

Louis Zamperini, Devil at My Heels: A Heroic Olympian's Astonishing Story of Survival as a Japanese POW in World War II

Man Overboard & Rescue at Sea

And now the rest of the Jim Devin story

(Transcribed and edited from an article in the San Diego Times Union dated Sunday Morning, April 20, 1969.)

2 HOURS IN SEA
Sailor Brushes Death off Japan
By: Jamie Bryson
There was a little something Machinist's Made third class Jim Devin, a husky six-foot, 200 pound sailor from Chula Vista, had to tell his wife, Janece, yesterday when Devin's ship came home from the Western Pacific. He told her while he and Mrs. Devin stood by a rail near where it happened last April 5, 60 miles off the coast of Southern Japan. "I fell overboard," said Devin, 22. "You didn't!" said Mrs. Devin, her eyes widening. "Well, I did," Devin said, "and I bobbed around in a big storm for two hours." He hadn't written to her about the incident, Devin told his wife of seven months, because he wanted to tell her of his brush with death in person.

OFF JAPAN

Devin said that his ship, the destroyer USS Porterfield (DD682), was in a storm off Japan and he had gone on deck to take pictures about 8 a.m. "It was real rough," he said. "The wind was blowing 45 miles an hour and the waves were 20 to 25 feet high. We were rolling around a lot." Devin said a particularly big wave washed the ship and when the water cleared, he saw a man apparently unconscious on the deck at the fantail.

MET CORPSMAN

"I went down to help him," Devin said. "Met the ship's hospital corpsman on the main deck and together we worked our way back to the fantail." The two reached the unconscious man, who later recovered from injuries he had suffered when he was throw-n against a railing by a giant wave. 'The next thing I knew, I was swimming," Devin said. With no lifejacket, Devin, in the Navy three years, resorted to a procedure he had learned in recruit training. "1 took off my trousers tied knots in the legs and inflated them with air by waving them over my head," he said. "It worked. They kept me afloat."

Meanwhile, the Porterfield and the guided missile destroyer John Paul Jones had started a search for Devin. "Ille chances of his being found in the storm were slight - 1,000 to one, an officer on the John Paul Jones said later. Devin watched as the ships criss-crossed the area for two hours searching for him.

Twice the John Paul Jones passed within 150 yards.

GRABS HOLD OF RAIL

"Finally the Jones came straight for me," said Devin. "I waved my arms like crazy and they saw me. Later, a lookout told me it looked like I was walking on the water. "Believe me, I was trying." Devin can't remember his first words as he was hauled over the railing of the John Paul Jones, where he was wrapped in a blanket, fed brandy and given dry clothes, "but it took five guys to break my grip on that rail," he said. "1 wasn't about to let go of that ship once I got hold." Devin was among more than 500 officers and men returning to San Diego Naval Station yesterday morning aboard the Porterfield and the destroyer Morton after six month deployments in the Vietnam combat zone.

WITH BATTLESHIP

The ships had been traveling until mid-week with the battleship New Jersey, which was bound home to Long Beach after a Vietnam tour, then was ordered to proceed instead to the area of North Korea. A homecoming for the New Jersey was canceled in Long Beach.

In his own words:

"As far as not being dangerous aboard ship, let me relate something to you. As we were steaming back from our cruise and heading home, we were caught up in a severe storm about 80 miles off Japan. I had gone topside with a friend when I noticed someone laying on the deck, not moving, with blood all around him. I told the guy with me to get the Hospital Corpsman while I went to help the injured man. As I came down the ladder to the main deck, the Corpsman just happened to come out through a watertight door. I grabbed him by the arm and started pulling him with me. We reached the injured man and I had just picked him up under the arms and the Corpsman had him by the legs, when the ship took a roll to starboard, the water hit, and the next thing I knew, I was swimming. In conditions like we were in, the ship has to maintain a high rate of speed and head directly into the swells. When the ship rolled, it was about 40 degrees to starboard. The water was about 50 degrees, the swells were 20-30 feet high and the wind was blowing at about 50 knots. Not the best conditions - and me without a life jacket!

My first thought - get away from the props or I was going to be fish food! My next thought was of my wife. We had just been married 37 days before we deployed. Then, I thought about sharks! I remembered something they taught us in boot camp use your pants as a flotation device! I'm here to tell you it works!! Approximately 2 hours later I was picked up by the USS John Paul Jones DDG-32. My ship had to proceed on to port because the Corpsman had sustained injuries after the last roll and now there was no one to administer first aid. So you see, you didn't have to be face to face with someone to die! Everyone who went has my eternal respect and support."

We have also found out that the injured man, the Oil King James Detlefsen, BTI, survived and is living in Oregon.

Man Overboard: The rest of the story

HM1	David L. Crabbe	Navy and Marine Corp Medal
MM2	David E. Lesh	Navy and Marine Corp Medal
MM3	James D. Devin	Navy and Marine Corp Medal
FN	Frankie M. Paxton	Navy and Marine Corp Medal
RD3	Mark R. McMaster	Navy Achievement Medal
SN	Robert W. Hampton	COMSEVENTHFLT Commendation
FN	Arthur D. Pacheco	COMSEVENTHFLT Commendation

While Machinist Mate Jim Devin was struggling in his own life and death battle with the raging sea, another life and death battle was being waged on the deck of USS Porterfield. Devin was one of a handful of sailors who unselfishly rushed to the aid of a stricken sailor badly hurt and laying bleeding and unconscious on the fantail of the ship.

Machinist Mate Dave Lesh tells of that battle.

Porterfield Event - April 5, 1969
As remembered by David Lesh - MM2 (April 27, 2015)

Conditions:

The ship had been in severe weather conditions for at least two days recording thirty-foot waves, high winds and taking rolls up to forty-five degrees. The bow would dive into a wave and the engine-room throttle men would have to cut back on the steam going to the main engines to prevent excessive cavitation when the stern would rise enough for the screws to begin coming out of the water. They would then immediately need to reopen the valves to bring the rpm's back up to maintain the ships intended speed once the stern settled back down. The bow often times would, at the same time, be coming completely out of the water, while the ship was taking heavy rolls. That process happened continuously.

Traversing the main deck was restricted to necessary movement only. The in-board life line was in place on the main deck. During a portion of this time the mess decks had to modify the meal service, because it could not provide some of the meals in a safe manner.

Example of movement:

In order to go from one of the aft compartments to the forward engine-room it was necessary to wait until the stern had risen almost to its maximum, open the hatch, look forward to see if it was safe to move forward, close and dog the hatch, go as fast as you could to get to the hatch leading to the engine-room. By then, the bow would be rising and the next wave would be on its way.

Prelude to the event:

I had stood watch, in the forward engine-room, from 0400 until 0745. After going to the mess decks, I went back to my bunk in the engineering compartment under gun mount 54. The crew was mustering in their respective compartments (also called foul weather mustering). When we were called to muster, Frank Paxton (FN) and I sat on the two ladders leading up to the enclosed space under the gun mount. Above us only the two man-hole hatches (zebra hatches) of the large hatch were open.

The event:

The starboard main deck hatch opened. I expected the hatch to close quickly and hear it being dogged down tight. When that didn't happen, I stood up on the ladder so that my head was above the hatch. The starboard hatch was still open and someone was laying across the threshold. I shouted to Paxton to give me a hand. I jumped up into the compartment and grabbed Dave Crabbe (HM-1) pulling him into the safety of the compartment. Paxton secured the hatch.

The compartment was in controlled kayos. The corpsman striker was tending the injured men with helpers and others gathered around. The remainder of the compartment was filled with men all talking at once about what had just happened.

It was at this time the alarm for man over board sounded. My first thought was that this was a mix up, because we had rescued Detlefsen. Then it became apparent that Jim Devin (MM-3) was missing. Arthur Pacheco (FN) had made it back to the compartment and was telling everyone about the wave that hit Crabbe, Devin and Detlefsen. He had been on the 01 level with Devin taking pictures of the storm, when they saw Detlefsen being washed down the main deck by a large wave slamming him against the starboard depth charge rack. Devin instructed Pacheco to contact the bridge and immediately went to Detlefsen's aid. He and the corpsman arrived just before a large wave crashed down on them. As the wave was subsiding, Pacheco saw that Devin had disappeared and Crabbe was injured. Pacheco continued to update the bridge about the events on the fantail including Devin going overboard.

The man overboard head count confirmed that we had a man missing, and that it was Jim Devin. At some point shortly after that, the XO came down into the compartment to get an update on the injured and to discuss what had happened.

With our only qualified corpsman semi-conscious with unknown issues and a man with compound fractures, being semi-conscious, bleeding and other unknown injuries, the captain had to make a hard decision relative to our injured shipmates and a man overboard. The decision was made to turn the search and rescue operation over to the U.S.S. John Paul Jones (DDG 32) and to proceed to a location alee of Japan to facilitate the transfer of the injured to a helicopter in order to expedite medical treatment.

Just after securing from the special sea and anchor detail, from the helo transfer, we received word that the John Paul Jones had rescued Devin. You can't imagine the joy that was felt aboard the Porterfield when the word was passed.

I have always looked back at the event marveling at the instantaneous decisions made and the results. For me, there will probably never be a luckier day in my life. This could have gone so wrong that instead of being able to talk about the positive actions taken by a group of people without concern for themselves, we could have very easily been talking about a catastrophe.

We hollered down below for assistance. Crabbe was cold, soaked and barely conscious. We tried to lift him and feed him down the hatch into the compartment below. He resisted. We tried again with the same result. Noticing that he was mumbling, I put my ear down near his mouth and told him to say it again. He needed to say it twice before hearing the word "outside." I repeated that back to him and he relaxed. Looking over at Paxton I said, "Someone else is out there." Without a second thought, he opened the starboard main deck hatch and went outside. Crabbe allowed me to hand him off to the waiting hands below, and I immediately followed Paxton out onto the deck.

While closing and dogging the hatch, I looked aft and saw Paxton arriving at a body up against the starboard depth charge rack. Then I took a look up the starboard side of the ship toward the bow and saw a wall of water (which I knew was at least twice my height) rolling towards us as the stern was going back down. Grabbing the in-board life line with my left hand, I started aft realizing that I would not get to them before the wave hit. So, I grabbed the life line with both hands and hung on. The wave knocked me off my feet spinning me at least once around the life line. I remember the water pressure in my ears increasing and decreasing as the wave passed over. Finally my head came above the water and I began pulling myself along the cable as the stern was again rising above the water.

To my amazement, both Paxton and Detlefsen (BT-1) were still there. There was blood on the deck with Detlefsen laying in a heap. There was no time to assess his injuries. We pulled him up with each of us grabbing his belt on either side. We turned toward the bow to begin our return to the enclosed portion of the ship, forward of the 55 gun mount.

The stern had started to go back down and we could see a wave approaching. At that point, I was the only one holding the cable. We were three abreast when the wave hit. It slammed us against the life line. I was holding the line with my right hand, Detlefen hit the line and Paxton was able to grab the line with his left hand as he was forced against it. We held on for dear life! The wave, again, spun us, the water was way over our heads knocking us off our feet, and yet Paxton and I were somehow able to hold on to both Detlefsen and the cable. The stern started back up and the water started to ebb. As soon as the water was down to our waists, we started forward. We reached the hatch before the next wave making it safely inside. Crew members were waiting to help. They took Detlefsen below. Paxton and I followed. The only person available to render assistance to the injured men was a corpsman striker (I can't recall his name).

Between the temperature of the water and the adrenaline flowing through my veins, I started shaking. Someone put a couple of blankets on me and it still took some time to warm up and calm down.

A Navy community at sea

A destroyer typically works in support of a Carrier Air Group (CAG)

Like this one which looks like it may be the Kitty Hawk

Underway Replenishment (UNREP)

The carriers supply fuel, food, ammunition, mail, movies and when necessary medical aid, to its escort vessels.

USS Enterprise (CVN-65)

Enterprise was the first nuclear powered aircraft carrier

USS Kitty Hawk (CVA-63)

Tin cans lined up for a turn at the gas pump

Heaving in and connecting up 'The Probe' - Refueling at sea (RASing) by passing lines between two ships and connecting the 'span wire' to a strong point on-board the receiving ship, at a distance of between 80 -120feet apart. The RAS Party would heave in on the 'hose line' and the probe would travel down the span wire until it slammed home in its receiving 'bell' housing. Once connected up, the engineers would start pumping and fill our tanks. Service was poor. No-one ever once offered to check the oil or wipe the windows! Ships in a combat or operational environment RASed daily or at least every 2'nd day and generally in the middle of the night!

Even the carriers went grocery shopping

This one had everything we needed - one stop shopping.

The bigger supply ships dropped in on us. Watching these big birds was like watching an aerial circus. Often this aerial dance occurred at the same time we were tethered to the supply ship taking on fuel.

Years later, on a luxury cruise, I met one of those pilots.

Bull Session

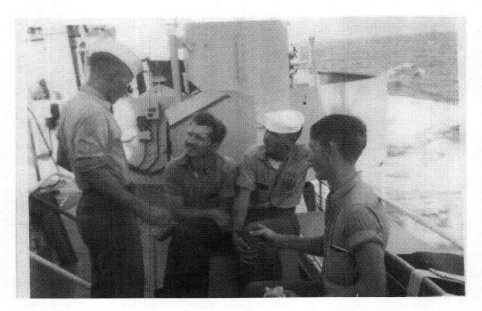

"I may not agree with what you say, but I will defend to the death your right to say it!"

Yea ... sometimes sailors talked like that.

I am a navy wife. I take no moment spent together for granted. I hold onto every touch, caress, kiss, every word. I have memorized the feel of his skin, his smell, the sound of his voice, and I play it over and over in my mind so that I will not forget. I cry myself to sleep some nights because missing him hurts so badly, but wake up the next morning, brush myself off, and start a new day.

Unknown

Plane Guard

This is why we were there

A destroyer coming into position for a "plane guard" assignment. The primary job here is to aid in rescue and recovery of aircrews who, for whatever reason, find themselves in the water. Unfortunately, in the one case we were called on for rescue ... the pilot did not survive and we had a valiant Navy pilot KIA (Killed in Action) on our deck.

An A-6 Intruder launching for a bombing mission

An F-8 combat pilot punching out following a landing mishap

A rescue swim team pulling in a downed pilot

Plane Guarding-A Hazardous Job

The news man who wrote the following served for three years on a US Navy destroyer that did frequent plane guard duly

By BOB MONROE Associated Press Writer NEW YORK (AP)

Plane guarding is one of the most exacting and hazardous assignments performed by destroyers in the course of fleet operations. The predawn collision between the Australian carrier Melbourne and the destroyer USS Frank E. Evans in the South China Sea emphasizes the danger involved in the assignment. Australian Navy Minister Clive Kelly told newsmen in Adelaide that the Evans was serving as plane guard to the Melbourne at the time of the collision. The hazard in plane guarding stems from the speed involved and the proximity in which the two ships must operate. The destroyer's role is to rescue the pilot if a plane goes into the sea either in taking off from the carriers deck or while trying to land. To conduct flight operations the carrier steams at top speed and heads into the wind to get the maximum relative wind from the wings of the aircraft. The destroyer takes up one of several prescribed positions relative to the carrier and oriented to the base course used for launching and retrieving planes. During flight operations a crew stands by one of the destroyer's motor whale boats which has been swung out over the water, ready to be lowered immediately in the event of an emergency. The challenge for the destroyer's Officer Of the Deck, OOD, is to keep station on the carrier as the larger ship changes course and speed.

Because of their difference in size, the carrier does not accelerate at the same rate as the destroyer or turn in the same radius and the destroyer's officer must use his experience and judgment in, calculating how rapidly to change speed and shift rudder.

A miscalculation may bring the ships dangerously close together or put the destroyer grossly out of station. Either situation is likely to bring a sharp rebuke from the carrier.

If the ships should suddenly come on collision course while changing station at high speed, there is very little time or space for evasive maneuvers.

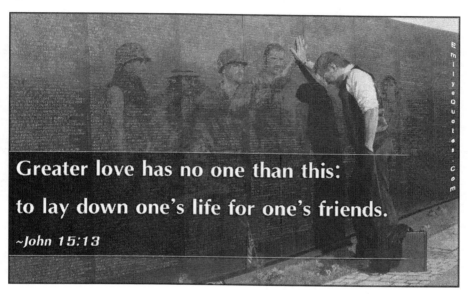

Greater love has no one than this: to lay down one's life for one's friends.
~John 15:13

Naval Gunfire support

This is a view of a gun fire support mission from the gun director, one of my duty stations. We had 5 of these 5" 38 caliber guns, and often would fire salvos of all guns

As I recall we had good accuracy out to 10+ miles.

Shown are the cases used for the 5" powder casings. Looks like this sailor had a busy day at the office.

There just seems to be a sort of simplistic beauty with those single gun turrets.

This is the Porterfield - mount 51 at the forward end of the ship. The fellow with the guitar and cigarette is Ernesto Gomez who I served with and met up with again at the reunion in 2013 and several times since. The other two are Erbe Clark and Bill Pankey.

During one of our 5 gun salvos, the shells cooked off in the barrels, damaging 4 of our 5 guns. I was on the elevation knob at the fire control computer at the time and entered two very large up spots prior to the "cease fire." No one was hurt.

This is why we were there!

The soldier wore a red shoulder patch indicating this unit is with the 1'st Infantry Division, the 'Big Red One', of the US Army.

In the trenches in Vietnam.

Even though tin cans gave much needed support to Marines and soldiers on the ground,

the Blue Water Navy was not immune to North Vietnamese shooting back.

Normandy: June 1944

With U.S. soldiers pinned down on Omaha Beach, American destroyers steamed in close to shore, opened fire on German positions, and helped turn the tide of invasion.

'The Navy Saved Our Hides'

Reprinted from Naval History with permission; Copyright 2014 U-S. Naval Institute/ww.v.usni.org.
By Craig L. Symonds

The first Allied soldier stepped ashore on Omaha Beach at 0640 on 6 June 1944, and immediately found himself in a virtual hell of machine-gun and artillery fire. "Drenching fire" from a naval bombardment, which was supposed to have softened up the beach and demoralized defenders, had been too brief. Bombs from hundreds of Allied aircraft had fallen inland well beyond the beach, and rockets from the rocket-firing LCTs (landing craft, tank) offshore had mostly landed too short.

As a result, the German defenders were able to emerge from their concrete bunkers and man the 85 machine-gun positions behind the beach and on both flanks and initiate a merciless fire. That made it impossible for naval combat demolition units (NCDUs) to disable or neutralize all of the many beach obstructions. As a result, despite months of careful planning and preparation, the men in the first several waves were targeted by fierce and relentless machine-gun fire.

By 0800, it had become a mess. Those soldiers who had landed, and those sailors forced to join them when their craft were wrecked, sheltered precariously and imperfectly behind a low ridge a few hundred yards inland from the surf line, their faces pressed into the smooth stones of the beach's shingle in a vain effort to avoid the machine-gun bullets passing only inches over their heads. Landing craft maneuvered awkwardly offshore vainly seeking a place to land along a beach crowded with still-extant obstacles and scores of burning or wrecked Allied landing craft. And all the while, the relentless tide continued to mount the beach, faster than some of the wounded could crawl, reducing slowly but inexorably the narrow strip of land where men could still live.

At 0830 the beachmaster on Omaha notified Rear Admiral John "Jimmy" Hall, who commanded the ships of "Force O" offshore, that "they were stopping the advance of follow up waves. " Only two hours after it had started, the invasion of Omaha Beach had stalled. Lieutenant General Omar Bradley, commander of the U.S. First Army, confessed later that he was contemplating "'evacuating the beachhead and directing the follow up troops to Utah Beach or the British beaches." Horrified by the prospect of failure, he asked Rear Admiral Alan G. Kirk, who commanded the Western (American) Naval Task Force, if there wasn't something more the Navy could do to break the bloody stalemate on Omaha Beach. As it happened, there was.

Destroyers to the Rescue
Most of the American destroyers that had participated in the early-morning bombardment of the beaches had retired offshore prior to H-hour, partly to make room for the landing craft and partly to take up screening positions to seaward. Nevertheless, the destroyer skippers could see for themselves that the situation on Omaha was deteriorating, and even without orders, some of them had returned to the beachfront to open fire on the high ground behind the beach. Now, just past 0830, Hall recalled the rest, ordering them to "'maintain as heavy a volume of fire on beach target[s] as possible." In support of that, Rear Admiral Carleton Bryant, commanding the big ships of the bombardment group off Omaha Beach, radioed a general message from the USS Texas (BB-35): "Get on them, men! Get on them! They are

raising hell with the men on the beach, and we can't have any more of that! We must stop.

The destroyer captains responded with enthusiasm—indeed, almost too much enthusiasm. Most of the responding ships were American Gleaves class destroyers that drew more than 13 feet of water, and the gradual slope of Omaha Beach made close-in fire support extremely hazardous. It was self-evident that if a destroyer grounded in the shallows, the German gunners could blast her to pieces at their leisure. Nevertheless, the destroyers now came speeding shoreward at 20 knots or more into water that was both unmarked and outside the mine-swept channels.

One sailor on board an LCT that was approaching the shore was shocked to see "a destroyer ahead of us with heavy smoke pouring from its stack." The ship appeared to be out of control and headed directly for the beach. "My God, " he thought, "they're going to run aground and be disabled right in front of the German artillery." At the last minute, the destroyer made a sudden hard left, turned her starboard side parallel to the beach, and began "blazing away with every gun it had, point blank at the defensive positions. " The sailor was thrilled to see "Puffs of smoke and mounds of dirt" flying "everywhere on the hillside as the destroyer passed swiftly by."

More than a dozen Allied destroyers responded to the call that morning, nine of them from Destroyer Squadron (DESRON) 18, under the command of U.S. Navy Captain Harry "Savvy" Sanders. Two of Sanders' destroyers, the Satterlee (DD-626) and "Thompson (DD-627) along with HMS Talybont, supported the U.S. Army Rangers assigned to assault the nearly vertical cliff at Pointe du Hoc west of Omaha Beach. Two more, the Carmick (DD-493) and McCook (DD-496), joined later by the Harding (DD-625), took up positions near the center of Omaha Beach off St. Laurent-sur-Mer, and five others, led by the squadron flagship Frankford (DD-497) with Sanders on board, steamed for the eastern end of the beach opposite Colleville-sur-Mer.

Most of the destroyers took up positions only 800 to 1,000 yards off the beach, so close that, as a newspaper correspondent reported, "Germans were hitting them with rifle bullets." Though the gradients varied across the beachfront, at that distance the water depth was only about 12 to 18 feet. Sanders later speculated that there were moments when the Frankford had only a few inches of water under her keel, and Kirk later asserted that "they had their bows against the bottom." Even if that were not literally true, it suggested the willingness of the destroyer captains to put their ships at risk in an obvious emergency.

These dozen or so destroyers constituted only a tiny fraction of the more than 5,000 ships that participated in the invasion of Normandy, but over the ensuing 90 minutes, they turned the tide of battle on Omaha Beach.

Aiding Army Rangers
Several destroyers also played a key role in what was perhaps the most daunting assignment of the entire invasion: the assault by 225 U.S. Army Rangers under Lieutenant Colonel James A. Rudder on Pointe du Hoc. Atop this nearly vertical cliff, the Germans were believed to have placed several heavy guns that could reach both of the American beaches—Omaha and Utah. To eliminate this threat, the Rangers would have to land on a narrow rocky beach at the base of the cliff, and then scale the cliff with ropes and ladders. Only 108 of the men who began the climb made it to the top. With so few of them, and arriving piecemeal as they did, their mission was touch and go. A crucial factor in their eventual success was gunfire support from the destroyers. Hard pressed by German light artillery, the Rangers used a blinker light to send target coordinates to the destroyers offshore. The Satterlee responded first, joined by the Thompson at 0830 and by the Ellyson (DD-454) an hour later. Unable to see the target, the destroyers

had to rely on indirect fire, stopping after each salvo to receive a report from the Rangers about the fall of shot. At 0952, the Rangers called for the destroyers to cease fire, and at 1130, lookouts in the destroyers saw an American flag flying over the position. Having scaled the cliffs, driven off the defenders, and seized the high ground, however, the Rangers soon discovered that the reported big guns on Pointe du Hoc had been removed, replaced by wooden dummies. They moved inland and set up a defensive perimeter, which they held for the rest of the day and into the night.

Trying to Find Targets
The other destroyers of Sanders' squadron, operating off Omaha Beach itself, had great initial difficulty identifying appropriate targets. The poor visibility along the beachfront and the excellent German camouflage made it all but impossible to figure out where the German guns were. Some of those guns retracted into underground bombproofs; others were so well hidden that, as one sailor put it, "you couldn't see it if you was ten feet from them. " In theory, the ships were supposed to coordinate with shore-based fire-control parties that would identify the targets and report the fall of the shot, as the Rangers did at Pointe du Hoc. But there was such chaos on the beach that morning and such a dearth of working radios that not until the afternoon did the destroyers establish regular radio communication with spotters ashore. In the meantime, the destroyer skippers were compelled to seek "targets of opportunity. " There was one immediate benefit of their arrival, however. Many of the German gunners, fearful of disclosing their location, briefly held their fire. Others shifted their fire to target the destroyers, and in either case, that created a blessed, if temporary, respite for the soldiers on the beach.

Near the center of Omaha Beach, just off the beachfront village of Les Moulins, Commander Robert Beer, the tall, lanky captain of the Carmick, scanned the bluffs looking for telltale '"puffs of smoke or flashes from enemy gun emplacements." Because the Germans were using smokeless powder, he saw none, and Beer became impatient, finding the process "'slow and unreliable." As he studied the beach through his binoculars, however, he noted a few Allied tanks trying vainly to fight their way up the draw, or gully, in the cliffs near Vierville-sur-Mer. It was evident to him that they were being held up by heavy gunfire from above, though he could not identify the source of that fire.

Several of the Allied tanks were shooting at a particular spot on the bluffs, and carefully noting the location, Beer directed his ship's guns to target those same positions. The Carmick fired a series of rapid-fire salvoes from her 5-inch guns into the suspicious area. After a few minutes, Beer saw that the tank gunners had shifted their fire to another site, and Beer directed his gunnery officer to follow suit. "It became evident," Beer reported afterward, "that the Army was using tank fire in [the] hope that fire support vessels would see the target and take it under fire." In a kind of deadly *pas de deux*, the tank men used their shells to point out enemy gun positions, and the destroyer men aimed accordingly.

Near the Carmick, Lieutenant Commander Ralph Ramey, in the McCook, opened fire on two strongly fortified German guns set into the cliff face. Many of Ramey's friends thought he was the spitting image of the comedian Will Rogers, and Ramey often sprinkled his conversation with country aphorisms, but he was all business now. Ramey and the McCook maintained an unremitting fire at the German battery for more than 15 minutes, and eventually that concentrated bombardment undermined the rock strata on which the enemy guns rested. The cliff crumbled away; one of the guns flew up into the air, and the other plunged down the cliff face.

A mile or two farther east, Commander Clarence Boyd, captain of the Doyle (DD-494), maneuvered his ship among the landing craft that were swarming off the Fox Green sector of Omaha Beach. From only 800 yards off the surf line, Boyd could see the men ashore "'dug in behind a hummock of sand along the beach, and the boats of the second wave [actually the third] milling around offshore." Absent contact with fire-control parties ashore, he posted lookouts to scan the high ground behind the beach for evidence of enemy gun positions, though visibility was "'very difficult because of smoke and dust in the target area. " One lookout reported a machine-gun emplacement on a steep hill at the west end of Fox Red Beach between *Colleville-sur-Mer* and *Le Grand Hameau,* and the Doyle fired two salvoes onto the site. The Doyle then shifted fire to a casemate at the top of the hill, fired two more salvoes, and in both cases, Boyd was able to report: "target destroyed."

More often, however, the results were less conclusive. Lacking other clear sightings, Boyd simply picked out what seemed to him to be logical places for gun positions to be and opened fire on them even if he could not see anything there. Having completed her assignment off Pointe du Hoc, the Thompson joined the Doyle off Fox Green Beach, and there her commander, Lieutenant Commander Albert Gebelin, whose darkly handsome features reminded some of a cigar-store Indian, directed his ship's fire into a clump of trees that he thought might be cover for a field battery. Whether it was or not, the trees got a thorough pounding. Other ships got into the act. A sailor on board an LCI' happened to be looking at the vegetation along the line of bluffs when he noticed a tiny movement among the bushes, and a second later a shell exploded on the beach. He kept his eye focused on those bushes, and soon another small movement of the brush was followed by another explosion on the beach. He called the skipper over and pointed it out. The officer watched as the pattern was repeated, and he noted the coordinates on his chart. He then got on the short-range TBS radio and called the nearest of the destroyers. Almost at once a destroyer "came barreling in there, popped over sideways, port side to the beach, and turned loose about eight rounds of 5-inch projectiles" into the German gun position.

Pounding the Enemy

Compared to the aerial bombs dropped from high altitude and the big shells fired by the battleships and cruisers from 10 or 15 miles offshore earlier that day, the smaller-caliber destroyer fire was more accurate and therefore far more effective. The morning's 8-, 12-, and 14-inch shells had made the ground shake, but they had left the German gun positions largely intact. Now those positions were pounded with hundreds of 5-inch shells and knocked out, one by one. One witness recalled seeing three 5-inch shells hit within 20 inches of a narrow gun slit in a pillbox, and in at least one case, a German artillery piece was hit directly on the muzzle and split wide open.

A beachmaster on Omaha, watching the "tin cans" fire into the cliff, later claimed, "You could see the trenches, guns, and men blowing up where they were hit. " There was no doubt in his mind that "the few Navy destroyers that we had there probably saved the invasion. " With more enthusiasm than precision, he insisted that the handful of American ships "'destroyed practically the entire German defense line at Omaha Beach. " If they didn't quite do that, they did change the trajectory of the battle. Inside an artillery bunker behind Omaha Beach, a German regimental commander phoned headquarters to report: "Naval guns are smashing up our strongpoints. We are running short of ammunition. We urgently need supplies. " There was no answer because the line had gone dead.

For more than an hour, from shortly before 0900 until well past 1000, the destroyer gunfire was virtually nonstop. And it needed to be. As a landing craft filled with 200 soldiers headed for the beach, her commanding officer noted that "1f a destroyer ceased shelling a shore battery for even a very brief time, the battery resumed fire on the craft along the beach."

Of course, the constant firing soon depleted the ammunition stores on board the destroyers. To ensure that they retained sufficient capability for emergencies, the Operation Neptune invasion order had specified that the destroyers were to expend no more than 50 to 60 percent of their ammunition before going back to England to replenish. In this crisis, however, the destroyer skippers disregarded that injunction. Gleaves class destroyers carried between 1,500 and 2,000 rounds of general purpose 5-inch ammunition. Most of the ships in Sanders' squadron had fired off between a quarter and a third of that during the morning bombardment, and now they expended most of what was left.

Between 0850 and 1015 that morning, the Emmons (DD-457) fired 767 rounds, the McCook fired 975, and the Carmick 1,127. Kirk became sufficiently nervous about this that he issued an order that "destroyers must husband [their] ammunition," reminding them, "our resources are limited. " When the gunners in the Herndon (DD-638) ran out of high-explosive ammunition, they began firing star shells, primarily used for illumination. On board the Butler (DD-636), Petty Officer Felix Podolak remembered that the firing was so hot *"We had to hook up one-and-a-half-inch fire hoses to hydrants to spray water on our gun mount,"* and even then, "the barrels were running red hot." The German gunners fired back, mostly with their mobile 88-mm guns, but the swift destroyers were difficult targets, even in the shallow and crowded waters off Omaha Beach. The destroyer skippers used their engines "in spurts, " ordering them alternately "ahead and astern, to throw off the enemy gunners. " There were some close calls. A German battery behind Fox Red Beach straddled the Emmons, and the Baldwin (DD-624) was hit twice in rapid succession, the first shell striking her whaleboat on the starboard side, and the second blowing an 8-by-12-inch hole in her main deck. But the Emmons escaped injury, and the Baldwin responded with accurate counterbattery fire, silencing her tormentor after several salvoes. No other destroyer was hit during this crucial and decisive 90-minute period along Omaha Beach.

Successes and Errors

Shortly before noon, the accuracy of the destroyer gunfire improved when the ships finally established contact with some of the fire-control parties ashore. At 1124 Army spotters directed the fire of the Frankford into a concentration of German troops behind the beach and beyond the sightline of the destroyers. After two salvoes, the spotters called a cease-fire because the soldiers had scattered.

Given the dearth of working radios ashore, and the complications of interservice communication, it is not surprising that there were errors. Late that afternoon, several of the American destroyers received reports that the Germans were using the church steeples in both Colleville-sur-Mer and Vierville-sur-Mer as observation posts. The Emmons took on the task of taking down the steeple in Colleville, and after a few salvoes, she did, smashing it, as one sailor recalled, "*just like you'd hit it with a big ax.*" A few miles to the west, off Vierville, the Harding took the church there under fire. From offshore the results looked spectacular. The Harding 's first salvo clipped off the cross at the peak, the second hit the steeple about ten feet from the top, and the third hit ten feet below that. From seaward it looked like the Harding was slicing off the steeple ten feet at a time, and Admiral Bryant, watching from the bridge of the Texas , thought it was "a beautiful sight." The reality on the ground was much different. Not only did the shelling cause a lot of collateral damage, but far worse, U.S. troops had already captured the town, and the Harding's shells killed and wounded a number of Americans. Army Captain Joseph of the 16th Infantry thought it was "totally disgraceful." Despite such errors, the cumulative effect of the close-in naval gunfire support was decisive. For the first time since they had landed, the men lying face-down behind the low rise of sand and shingle at the high-tide mark were able to lift their heads and look around them for a way off the beach. As early as 1036, lookouts on board the

Frankford noted that some Allied troops were beginning to advance, moving forward from that low hillock of sand toward the base of the cliffs. And an hour later, at 1137, some of the German defenders began coming out of their positions with their hands up. While much of this was the result of incredible bravery and determination by the soldiers themselves, the destroyers played a critical role. In his postwar memoir, Bradley acknowledged that "the Navy saved our hides."

That is why we were there!

US Navy: A Global Force for Good!

The United States is considered by many of us to be an "Exceptional Nation." The following pages show part of that heritage.

As many of us know from personal family history, multitudes came to this nation to escape tyranny in their home countries, and also to avail themselves of the opportunities provided by America under its Constitution where "We the people" is the operative directive.

Very quickly following the founding of this nation it became an economic powerhouse rivaling many of the long-established nations and empires of Europe. The growing economy further encouraged more immigration from many parts of the world and the nations growth necessitated increasing economic and military obligations in various parts of the world.

Our military has been a key part of this exceptionalism, and a good place to begin such talk is the conclusion of the Civil War. The southern confederacy had been defeated on the battle field at tremendous cost to both sides, and the two commanding generals, Ulysses S. Grant and Robert E. Lee met at the Appomattox Courthouse to conclude the hostilities. Lee was understandably very nervous about this meeting both for the safety of himself and for his soldiers. You see, it was quite common throughout history for the defeated soldiers, and especially the defeated leaders, to be taken captive and marched in humiliation through the victor's capital city. Often, they were executed following the humiliation of defeat and capture.

But something quite different happened at the courthouse that day. General Grant treated General Lee with dignity and respect. Following the formalities of the surrender, Grant offered Lee and his soldiers pardons for their criminal and treasonous actions. The southern soldiers and their officers, including Lee, were sent home with the admonition to help rebuild the nation as one nation. An exceptional action by an exceptional nation. I have been carrying a copy of that pardon in my wallet for years as a reminder

We see the exceptional actions of our military often down through the years. Disasters of all sorts in all parts of the world are met typically with massive help, often via US Navy ships and their crews, including the Marines.

The aftermath of World War Il, with the Germans and Japanese fully and completely defeated at great cost to the world, shows the exceptionalism of our nation.

In both cases, in Europe and Japan, American foreign policy was instrumental and vital to the reconstruction and rehabilitation of those former enemies. The rehabilitation included the establishment of a constitutional and representative form of government.

In the years following World War Il, American military presence protected those rebuilding countries of Europe and Asia and acted as the chief foil against a new and growing world threat the threat of Communism from the Soviet Union and China who sought to impose their will on the world.

The aftermath of the Vietnam war continued to show the exceptionalism of America, in particular American, military as we will see in the following stories.

In the twentieth century it is estimated that Communism killed close to 100 million people, and Nazism another 25 million. The United States and its allies pushed back against these totalitarian systems that sought to enslave the world. American sailors can take pride in preserving liberty throughout the world.

Pictured are some of the estimated 2 million Vietnamese boat people escaping the oncoming tyranny of Communist North Vietnam. Many, perhaps most, perished in their attempted escape to freedom.

South Vietnamese people attempting escape from the coming Communist invasion from the North.

Some of the 2 million Korean refugees at Pusan South Korea, escaping North Korean and Chinese tyranny and death.

Gene Beckstrom, a WW-II tin-can sailor and a friend, joined the Navy at 16 and served in many of the South Pacific naval battles of WW-II. He then served an additional 20 years in the Army, including 2 combat tours in Korea with the 76'th and 25'th Combat Engineering Divisions.

Gene tells of one particular battle where he and only two others of his company survived.

Following his military service, Gene became a Christian pastor and over the past 25 years has started 19 churches in the remote northern Minnesota area.

Here is the Chaos in South Vietnam following US Congressional withdrawal of American support. The loss of support resulted in perhaps 1 million lives lost in South Vietnam, and subsequently 2 million in Cambodia (one third of the population) when the dictator Pol Pot met no resistance to his atrocities.

SHIP THAT RESCUED FAMILY AT SAIGON'S FALL BEGAN LIFE IN US NAVY

> *The author talking again:* Ya know Mom ... I've shared with you some pretty scary and awful things so far. But there's more to the sailor's stories than that. Often times we were able to come to the aide of people in much trouble ... trouble that threatens their lives and freedoms. Natural disasters in which we provide much needed help and aide. And then there are stories of the rescue of people caught up in the horrors of war such as the two stories which follow - Bittersweet events, but in the end very heartwarming as we see lives saved and changed for the better.

By Jeanette Steele. April 29, 2014 San Diego Union Tribune

South Vietnamese frigate Tran Hung Dao, the former U.S. destroyer escort Camp (DE-251), which served in the Atlantic and Pacific during World War Il.

A boat was at the pier. That's all Minh Nguyen's family knew on April 29, 1975, the frantic final day before the fall of Saigon.

Nguyen, just 2 years old at the time, clung to his father's

back as the entire extended family scrambled and clawed their way onto the barricaded pier and up cargo nets into that ship.

The vessel, loaded almost to the sinking point with fleeing South Vietnamese, delivered them to safety and freedom.

Nguyen has known the outline of his family's evening escape. The detail he didn't know was the ship itself.

That South Vietnam-flagged vessel started a thread that would run through Nguyen's life without him realizing it.

It's a uniquely Southern California story, bound up with the U.S. Navy in San Diego and Orange County's large Vietnamese-American population.

The ship brought Nguyen and his family to the Philippines. They next went to a refugee camp in Guam, then to Iowa for five years and finally to Irvine. After graduating from college in 1994, Nguyen sought a way to pay for medical school without burdening his parents, who made a life for their five children by working odd jobs and eventually owning a gas station and pursuing other enterprises. The Navy provided a path, and Nguyen took it. He is the only member of his family to serve in U.S. colors. Assignments at the San Diego Naval Medical Center in Balboa Park and Miramar Marine Corps Air Station brought him to San Diego for the entirety of his 8-1/2 year Navy career. That tenure included him deploying in 2001 as a medical officer aboard the amphibious ship Ogden. Then, last year, Nguyen noticed a new photograph on the wall of his parents' home. It hung in a place of honor, right next to the family portrait.
The picture showed a ship bearing South Vietnam's flag. As a Navy man, Nguyen realized immediately that it was a warship — a warship that started its life flying the Stars and Stripes.

The boat that took his family to safety was the former U.S. destroyer escort Camp, which served in the Atlantic and Pacific during World War Il.

Re-designated as a radar picket ship, Camp patrolled off Cuba during the start of the Cold War and then in the Pacific as the Vietnam conflict heated up. The United States transferred the ship to South Vietnam in February 1971. It was renamed the Tran Hung Dao, a frigate in the Republic of Vietnam navy.

Nguyen was stunned. Suddenly, his naval service took on an entirely new dimension.

"It's such a small world. Now, 39 years later, it really makes me proud that I was part of the Navy and the role that it played in my family, in helping us leave at that time, " said Nguyen, currently an occupational medicine doctor and vice president at U.S. HealthWorks Medical Group in San Diego.

Growing up in Orange County, Nguyen remembers the large demonstrations there on each anniversary of the April 30 fall of Saigon. Emotions in that community (Orange County has 184,000 Vietnamese-American residents, the largest enclave outside Vietnam) include bitterness about the way the war ended. Despite massive US military evacuations of people via cargo plane and helicopter, the last Americans to depart Saigon left behind 400 Vietnamese at the U.S. Embassy alone.

Panicked South Vietnamese tried other methods as communist forces rolled into the city. Nguyen's family members knew they could not stay. Nguyen's father was a soldier in the South Vietnamese army; his mother's nephew served in the South Vietnamese navy.

That's how the fall of Saigon looked from inside.

Elmus Billingsley Jr. was a 20-year-old sailor on the Oklahoma City, a light cruiser assigned to protect the city's refugees as they poured into the waters off Saigon.

Billingsley, now an Escondido resident, said the details are still absolutely clear to him. He could hear explosions as the North Vietnamese army bombed targets in Saigon. People fled the city in nearly anything they could find, including tiny, non-motorized sampan boats. Some even swam and the Oklahoma City's small launches scooped them out of the water.

U.S. and South Vietnamese helicopters flew out to the Oklahoma City and several other U.S. Navy ships nearby to disgorge their passengers.

This last-ditch evacuation, called Operation Frequent Wind, saved an estimated 7,000 people after U.S. airplanes were forced to stop flying in and out of Saigon because Tan Son Nhat airfield suffered heavy bombing.

So many helicopters wanted to land on the ships that American sailors pushed empty aircraft off the decks to make room. Other pilots were ordered to drop their passengers onboard, then ditch their aircraft in the water.

Billingsley said watching helicopters being pushed overboard on the nearby command ship Blue Ridge was a surreal sight — like most of that momentous stretch of days.

Sailors slept out on deck so they could give their mattresses to refugees.

"These people had their backs up against a wall and were trying to get away from the North Vietnamese by any means necessary. We were their last hope" said Billingsley, a gunner's mate who retired in 1993 after 20 years in the Navy.

*"It was intense, "*he said. *"Everybody sort of felt sorry for what they were going through. We were glad to be there to help."*

Billingsley, now 59, often wonders what happened to the 154 refugees who came aboard the Oklahoma City. One woman gave birth in the ship's sick bay.

"I'm really, really humbled to have the things I have, compared to the things they left behind," he said.

Nguyen's parents didn't dwell much on the fall of Saigon — never participating in the anti-communist rallies in Orange County. They preferred to concentrate on their children's future.

All five Nguyen children have prospered. Minh, the youngest child and the only physician, is married to another Vietnamese refugee. The couple have two children, ages 9 and 7.

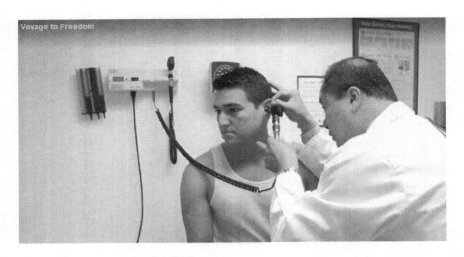

Nguyen's own kids know about his Navy background. They've seen photos of him in uniform, and both were born at the Balboa Park hospital.

The former Navy officer said it's perhaps the right moment to tell his children about their other history and the significance of the fall of Saigon.

"As my kids get older, I think it's time to share with them things like that," Nguyen said. *"I really try to find a way to emphasize to them how fortunate they are."*

"Things aren't always like this," he added, gesturing around his orderly medical office, where a photograph of the life-saving frigate Tran Hung Dao now hangs on the wall.

Ellis Island -1905

Valor at the Vietnam war's end:
The USS Kirk (DE-1087)

And then Mom ... there is the story of the USS Kirk.

When the US Congress cut off funding for the South Vietnam government, it was only a matter of time before the North Vietnamese military would roll into and conquer South Vietnam.
This left many desperate and fearful of their lives and the lives of friends and family.

Many of these desperate people were former military or government workers, allies of the US and would be shown no mercy by the invaders from the north.

Thousands were evacuated by US helicopters to offshore ships, but many more attempted escape to the sea by any means available ... including many overcrowded and unpowered vessels. Many died during this hurried and ad-hoc evacuation into the sea, and many thousands more died on-shore at the hands of the North Vietnamese.

The USS Kirk was in a supporting role in this "Frequent Wind" evacuation mission, and it was a big surprise when many South Vietnamese Huey helicopters and one very large twin rotor Chinook helicopters started showing up and wanting to land on the Kirk's small ASW drone landing deck with their load of desperate refugees.

"We looked up out on the horizon, and pretty soon all you could see were helicopters. And they came in and it was incredible. I don't think I'll ever see anything like it again," said Hugh Doyle, the chief engineer, now retired and living in Rhode Island.

Some 200 refugees were rescued from 16 helicopters by the Kirk's crew over a day and a half. The sailors looked after their Vietnamese visitors, over half of whom were women, children and babies. They put up tarps on the deck, so they would have some shelter from the blazing sun. They distributed food and water and played games with the children. The ship's crew found themselves changing diapers, treating wounds and giving comfort.

The crew of the Kirk had trained for and expected to be at war when they arrived for duty in the South China Sea off Vietnam. Instead, what was happening was a huge evacuation mission involving many American ships and helicopters.

Right away the crew knew a radically different mission was at hand.

"What was needed was a heart and a hand" as one sailor put it.

And the many children found comfort in the caring arms of toughened sailors.

Chief Hospital Corpsman Stephen Burwinkle carefully and professionally tended to the many medical needs of the new 'crew members' including the pregnant ladies.

This is the fear and chaos from which they were escaping.

The mission changes.

The Kirk reached Con Son Island, off the southern coast of Vietnam, on May 1, 1975. There, it was met by 30 South Vietnamese navy ships and dozens of fishing boats and cargo ships — and as many as 30,000 Vietnamese refugees.

"They were rusty, ugly, beat up," says Chipman. *"Some of them wouldn't even get under way; they were towing each other ... "*

Paul Jacobs, the captain of the Kirk, received the directive from Adm. Donald Whitmire, commander of the evacuation mission - Operation Frequent Wind. Jacobs recalls Whitmire's surprise message: *"He says, 'We're going to have to send you back to rescue the Vietnamese navy. We forgot 'em. And if we don't get them or any part of them, they're all probably going to be killed."*

The Kirk was being sent to an island off the Vietnamese mainland — alone.

The journey from South Vietnam to Subic Bay in the Philippines took 6 days.

Of the 30,000+ refugees on vessels escorted by the Kirk over six days, only three died.

 Using whatever vessel he could commandeer, Chief Stephen Burwinkel (Doc) traveled daily from ship to ship in the 30-ship convoy and held sick call to minister to the many medical needs of his 30,000 patients.

During the crossing to the Philippines, people soon became sick in the cramped ships. Stephen Burwinkel, the Kirk's medic — in the Navy he's called a hospital corpsman — went from ship to ship attending to those with dysentery, dehydration, diarrhea and other illnesses.

"When they gave me the meritorious service medal over all this, I quite frankly referred to it as my 'no-sleep' medal," says Burwinkel, who made a career in the Navy and is now retired and living in Pensacola, Fla. *"I would go out there and do my thing and at dark we would come back to the Kirk and try to get a little bit to eat and make some rounds —gather my wits about me, resupply myself and get ready for the next day."*

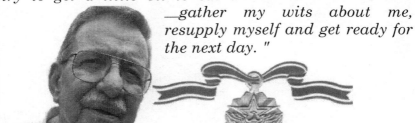

But as the flotilla approached the Philippines, the Kirk's captain got some bad news. The presence of South Vietnamese vessels in a Philippine port would present the government in Manila with a diplomatic predicament. *"The Philippine government wasn't going to allow us in, period, because these ships belonged to the North Vietnamese now and they didn't want to offend the new country,"* Jacobs, the captain, recalls.

The government of Philippine President Ferdinand Marcos was one of the first to recognize the Communist rulers now in control of a single Vietnam, and Jacobs was told the ships should go back.

Richard Armitage and his South Vietnamese friend, Capt. Do, came up with a solution that Marcos had to accept.

"We will raise the American flag and lower the Vietnamese flag as a sign of transfer of the ship back to the United States, because during the war those ships are given to the Vietnamese government as a loan, if you want, from the United States, to fight the Communists. Now the war is over, we turn them back to the United States."

"That was the last vestige of South Vietnam. And when those flags came down and the American flags went up, that was it. Because a Navy ship is sovereign territory and so that was the last sovereign territory of the Republic of Vietnam,"

Rick Sautter - a Kirk officer who took command of a Vietnamese ship.

"What was needed was a heart and a hand"

For the refugees, it was just the beginning of their long journey, which took them to Guam and then resettlement in the United States.

For the sailors of the Kirk, ending the Vietnam War by rescuing 20,000 to 30,000 people was very satisfying.

Reunion some 30+ years later

Ba Nguyen, here with his wife, Nho, was able to maneuver his helicopter so his passengers — including his 10-month-old daughter — could drop to safety on the Kirk. He then flew the Chinook over the ocean and jumped out while the helicopter crashed.

In the reunion years later, Kirk crew members honored Nguyen with an Air Medal, the award the U.S. military gives for heroic feats while flying. Though he is afflicted with advanced Alzheimer's, he saluted upon receiving the award.

" ... But most of all I will never forget the experience on USS Kirk and the crew members ... and a frigate named USS Kirk has always been in my thought, and from the bottom of my heart I would like to say thank you. Thank you for this wonderful country with wonderful people.

May God protect you and your family.

And God bless America. "

This lady gave her daughter the middle name "Kirk"

"These people were coming out of there with nothing. Whatever they had in their pockets or hands. Some of them had suitcases; some of them had a bag. You could tell they'd been in a war. They were still wounded. There were people young, old, army guys with the bandages on their head, arms - you could tell they'd been in a fight."

Kent Chipman was 21 when he served aboard the USS Kirk.

The Leaders

Commander Paul Jacobs retired from the Navy in 1984 as a captain after commanding three ships and serving as the U.S. Navy's Director of Undersea Surveillance. He is now President/CEO of Veteran Resources Corporation in Fairfax, Virginia.

Captain Kiem Do was deputy chief of staff for operations in the South Vietnamese Navy when Saigon fell in April 1975. After settling in the United States, he taught high school math and science and also worked as a cost engineer with a Louisiana utility company before he retired in 1997. He resides in Mandeville, Louisiana.

Richard Armitage has held many government positions since Vietnam, including Deputy Assistant Secretary of Defense, Assistant Secretary of Defense, and Deputy Secretary of State. He is currently president of Armitage International in Arlington, Virginia.

These are the faces of American Exceptionalism!

Liberty ... Respect ... Opportunity

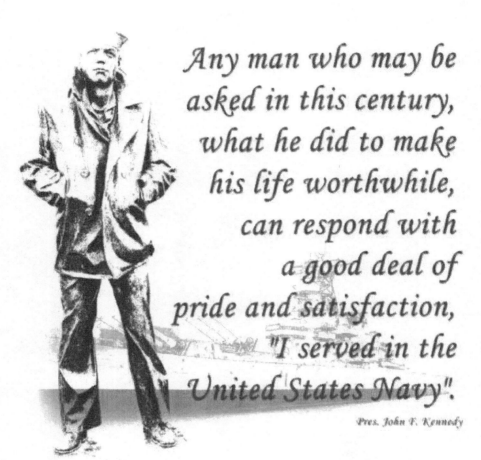

The Hell of battle damage

I'm tempted to end this here Mom ... with the heartwarming stories of rescue. But I must complete the stories I set out to tell.

Here's another of those stories Mom ... one I didn't want to worry you with, but a story of heroes worth telling

Stories of the USS Strong
- Victim of a torpedo attack

The following narrative is taken from:
http://destroyerhistory.org/fletcherclass/index.asp?r=46703&pid=46706

You may recall that we were operating as part of Task Force 36.1 with a mission of providing cover operations for a night landing of Marines in the vicinity of Rice Anchorage, New Georgia Island. Strong was in company of three cruisers, Honolulu, St. Louis and Helena, and three other destroyers, Nicholas, O'Bannon and Chevalier. We had been directed to bombard shore installations around Bairoko Harbor.

At about 0019 on 5 July, course was changed to 190 with ships in column for bombardment of targets on Kolombangara Island. The order of ships in column was: Nicholas, Strong, Honolulu, Helena, St. Louis, O'Bannon and Chevalier. At about 0028, Strong commenced firing to suppress firing from shore batteries. At about 0034, course was changed to 090 and firing was commenced on Bairoko Harbor. At about 0034, Strong ceased firing and changed course to 000 to pass Rice Anchorage and exit Kula Gulf with the task force. Strong had fired approximately 300 rounds of 5-inch ammunition during the bombardment. The PBY "Black Cat" air spotter had reported good results.

At about the time of course change to 000, the underwater sound equipment picked up extremely loud underwater noises that sounded something like locomotives traveling at great speed. These sounds were of about equal strength from three main directions— from the starboard bow in the direction of Rice Anchorage, from just forward of the port beam and from the starboard quarter. The sound stack operator, Jack Haley SOM 2/c, reported that this noise didn't sound like the training records, but he'd bet there were some damned big torpedoes around there someplace—going like hell. Lcdr. Purdy, the executive officer, pointed out that the noises were coming from everywhere and were loudest from the direction of Rice Anchorage—which was true. He said that they were probably associated with the landing and then dashed out of the CIC/charthouse onto the bridge. (It can only be conjectured that the noises appeared to "come from everywhere" because of reflections and reverberations from underwater coral formations in the very deep waters of the gulf.)

Lt(jg) Curran, the gunnery officer, states that just as Strong completed the bombardment of Bairoko and was turning to course 000 degrees, he looked to port and saw the phosphorescent wake of a torpedo headed for Strong. He switched to the JA circuit and yelled "Left ... " The words "full rudder" were masked by the explosion.

CAPTAIN
Immediately after Chevalier separated a few yards, Strong began to settle rapidly with the starboard list increasing to 40—60 degrees. Captain Wellings attempted to make his way down the outside inclined ladder leading from the after side of the bridge to the superstructure deck, but he was blocked by water when he was only one-third of the way down. He then went back to the starboard wing of the bridge and stepped into the water from the wind screen outboard of the starboard torpedo director. He was accompanied by L.A. Rodrigos, CQM, who remained with the captain throughout.

SUMMARY OF THE DAMAGE
The ship immediately assumed a starboard list of about 15 degrees, and from the "sag" amidships it was evident that the keel was broken.

Main power was lost throughout the ship immediately, but after a momentary delay, emergency power switched on and remained on as long as the ship was manned. All main battery guns were shifted to emergency power except 5-inch gun number 5. All guns were shifted to local control with orders from the gunnery officer not to fire on any target unless designated by the gunnery officer. The SG radar came back on line as soon as emergency power was available and continued to operate on relative bearings because of loss of gyro input. The radar effectiveness on surface targets was limited to targets that might be ahead and astern because of the large starboard list on the ship.

Internal communications generally were excellent. Sound powered phone communications were maintained with most stations until the word was passed to abandon ship. As for external communications, the receivers continued to function, but the transmitters were out. Attempts were made to report the torpedoing over TBS, "Black Cat" and Task Force frequencies but all transmitters were inoperative. A flashing light message was sent to Chevalier and was relayed to the task group commander.

A large hole was torn in the port side and main deck in the vicinity of frame 90. The deck plates were buckled between frames 75 and 105. The superstructure deck house collapsed on the port side between the after side of number one stack and the forward torpedo mount base ring. The boat winch was gone. Number 2 motor whaleboat was torn apart; one half of the boat dangled from the forward davit.

Number one fire-room was a shambles. This fire-room flooded immediately. The bulkhead between the forward fire-room and forward engine room was blown away. The engine room was totally disrupted, but further assessment of the damage was impossible because this space also flooded immediately. Seams were opened on the starboard side of the bulkhead between the forward engine room and after fire-room. The lower level flooded rapidly. Before the crew left the fireroom, they secured the stops on number three boiler. Just before the ship sank, the safety valves lifted on this boiler. The after-engine room was not flooded.

One fire was extinguished. Steam pressure was lost immediately. Shortly thereafter, the assistant engineering officer, Lt(jg) R.E. Trost, secured the after-engine room for towing. The bulkhead stops were secured, and the jacking gear was engaged.

The captain was about 25 yards from the ship and wearing a kapok life jacket when the ship sank. An instant before the sinking, the ship broke up with the after-end twisting to starboard. The captain was lying on his back when the first underwater explosion occurred. He felt terrific vibrations but was unaware of any follow-on explosions.

A few minutes later, he and Rodrigos spotted a float net nearby, thanks to the illumination from Japanese star shells. They attempted to paddle to Rice Anchorage with their hands. During the night, they picked up two enlisted men and one officer, Lt(jg), SC, Keith N. Sherlie, USNR. At about 0510, the group was rescued by USS Gwin. The captain and CQM Rodrigos suffered internal injuries from the underwater explosion and were hospitalized for a time.

Most of us in Strong felt an intense sadness at the loss of the ship. Certainly, all of the "old" hands believed they had a part to play on a ship of uncommon capabilities. No matter how intense our feelings were about the loss of the ship, they must have paled into insignificance when compared to those of the captain. He had commissioned the ship as commanding officer, had built real capabilities out of green recruits, had instilled unusually high morale, had developed unit self-confidence under fire—and, up until the final hour, had every reason to hope that Strong might become a legend in her own time. Now it was all sinking from under him through cruel circumstance. Yet he stood calmly among the crumbling ruin as a symbol of order, looking after the welfare of others with such fragments of control as may still come to hand. Finally, having given that last full measure within the means and time available, as the ship sank beneath his feet, he stepped off into the dark and waiting ocean. This must stand for all time among the great examples of self-control and leadership in adversity.

EXECUTIVE OFFICER

After Lcdr. Frederick Purdy left the CIC/chartroom for the bridge his actions are unknown until he appeared on the forecastle to take charge of rigging for tow. (At one time it was thought that O'Bannon was coming alongside to take us in tow.) Lcdr. Purdy remained forward with Lt(jg) Milt Hackett, Ens Jack Howard—and, at the last minute, possibly Lt(jg) Albert E. Oberg. This group devoted its efforts to helping as many of the crew as possible to get aboard Chevalier. They were still trying to get more men over when Chevalier backed away just before Strong sank. The ship sank out from under this group and they were in the water when Strong exploded.

Milt Hackett believes that he and Lcdr. Purdy were in close proximity until he (Milt) and Lt(jg) Fulham left to get help from the US forces at Rice Anchorage. After they were about 3/4 mile from the float net, a small Japanese landing craft came out from Kolombangara and shot many of the survivors in the water. It has been conjectured that Lcdr. Purdy was among the victims. Lcdr. Purdy's body was found by Robert F. Gregory, S1/c, and his small group of survivors on Kolombangara. Gregory later turned Purdy's wallet over to the Marines on New Georgia.

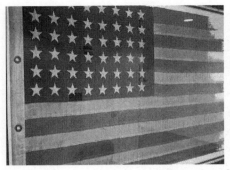

The 48-star battle ensign of the destroyer escort USS Samuel B. Roberts (DE-413), a legendary ship in a small, overmatched American force of escort carriers, destroyers, and destroyer escorts who fought off a massive Japanese battle fleet.

USS Yorktown (CV-5) being abandoned by her crew after she was hit by two Japanese Type 91 aerial torpedoes, 4 June 1942 during the Battle of Midway.

USS Balch (DD-363) is standing by at right. Note oil slick surrounding the damaged carrier, and inflatable life raft being deployed off her stern. Warren Seward and Sam Thomas, shipmates we met at the 2013 Balch/Porterfield reunion were aboard the Balch during this battle.

View of damaged rear twin 5-inch gun turret on board destroyer USS Higbee damaged by North Vietnamese MIG attack off the coast of North Vietnam. Higbee was the fourth ship damaged by Red attacks in recent days (AP).

I remember distinctly the first time I heard the announcement "General quarters, general quarters, THIS IS NOT A DRILL ... " Aircraft were coming at us from North Vietnam, and at the time we didn't know if they were friend or foe. A chill went up my back and I knew we were at war.

For years following my Vietnam tour, I thought we "blue water" sailors were safe from enemy fire. Only recently I discovered that 29 American ships received damage from North Vietnamese artillery fire and one MiG bombing attack. Nineteen of these ships received major damage requiring them to be taken off the line and sent to the yards for repair. No ships were lost but some lives were lost.

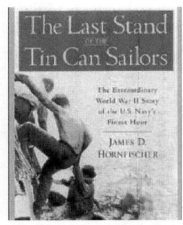

Photo # NH 96011 USS Samuel B. Roberts at sea, October 1944

I must take you back to the USS Samuel B. Roberts

"This will be a fight against overwhelming odds from which survival cannot be expected. We will do what damage we can."

With these words, Lieutenant Commander Robert W. Copeland addressed the crew of the destroyer escort USS Samuel B. Roberts on the morning of October 25, 1944, off the Philippine Island of Samar. On the horizon loomed the mightiest ships of the Japanese navy, a massive fleet that represented the last hope of a staggering empire. All that stood between it and Douglas MacArthur's' vulnerable invasion force were the Roberts and the other small ships of a tiny American flotilla poised to charge into history.

James D. Hornfischer paints an unprecedented portrait of the Battle off Samar, a naval engagement unlike any other in U.S. history—and captures with unforgettable intensity the men, the strategies, and the sacrifices that turned certain defeat into a legendary victory.

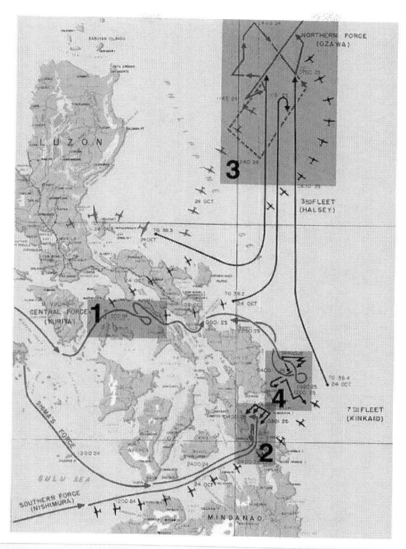

The four main actions in the battle of Leyte Gulf: 1 Battle of the Sibuyan Sea 2 Battle of Surigao Strait 3 Battle of (or 'off') Cape Engaño 4 Battle off Samar. Leyte Gulf is north of 2 and west of 4. The island of Leyte is west of the gulf.

The **Battle off Samar** (source: Wikipedia) was the centermost action of the Battle of Leyte Gulf, one of the largest naval battles in history, which took place in the Philippine Sea off Samar Island, in the Philippines on October 25, 1944. As the only major action in the larger battle where the Americans were largely unprepared against the opposing forces, it has been cited by historians as one of the greatest military mismatches in naval history.

> *"In no engagement of its entire history has the United States Navy shown more gallantry, guts and gumption than in those two morning hours between 0730 and 0930 off Samar"*— Samuel Eliot Morison, History of United States Naval Operations in World War Il, Volume MI, Leyte

Adm. William Halsey, Jr. was lured into taking his powerful 3rd Fleet after a decoy fleet, leaving only three escort carrier groups of the 7th Fleet in the area. A Japanese surface force of battleships and cruisers, battered earlier in the larger battle and thought to have been in retreat, instead turned around unobserved and stumbled upon the northernmost of the three groups, Task Unit 77-4-3 ("Taffy 3"), commanded by Rear Admiral Clifton Sprague. Taffy 3's few destroyers and slower destroyer escorts possessed neither the firepower nor armor to effectively oppose the Japanese force, but nevertheless desperately attacked with 5 inch/38 caliber guns and torpedoes to cover the retreat of their slow "'jeep" carriers. Aircraft from the carriers of Taffy 1, 2, and 3, including FM-2 Wildcats, F6F Hellcats and TBM Avengers, strafed, bombed, torpedoed, rocketed, depth-charged, fired at least one .38 caliber handgun and made numerous "dry" runs at the attacking force when they ran out of ammunition.

Sprague's task unit lost two escort carriers, two destroyers, a destroyer escort and dozens of aircraft. Over a thousand

Americans died, comparable to the combined losses of American men and ships at the better-known Battles of the Coral Sea and Midway. But in exchange for the heavy losses for such a small force, they sank or disabled three Japanese cruisers and caused enough confusion to persuade the Japanese commander, Vice Admiral Takeo Kurita, to regroup and ultimately withdraw, rather than advancing to sink troop and supply ships at Leyte Gulf. In the combined Battle of Leyte Gulf, 10,000 Japanese sailors and 3,000 Americans died. Although the battleship Yamato and the remaining force returned to Japan, the battles marked the final defeat of the Japanese Navy, as the ships remained in port for most of the rest of the war and ceased to be an effective naval force.

Freedom is never more than one generation away from extinction. We didn't pass it to our children in the bloodstream. It must be fought for, protected, and handed on for them to do the same, or one day we will spend our sunset years telling our children and our children's children what it was oncen the United States where men were free.

 The Battle of Midway, June 1942 USS Yorktown (CVS) is hit on the port side, amidships, by a Japanese Type 91 aerial torpedo during the mid-afternoon attack by planes from the carrier Hiryu, 4 June 1942.

Photographed from USS Pensacola (CA-24).

Yorktown is heeling to port and is seen at a different aspect than in other views taken by Pensacola, indicating that this is the second of the two torpedo hits she received. Note very heavy anti-aircraft fire.

A sailor's view of an incoming kamikaze.

Gene Beckstrom tells of how one day he was taking a break and sitting on a hatch looking out over the ocean when a kamikaze flew up beside the ship.
"I remember to this day" says Gene, "we looked at one another ... eyeball to eyeball. I thought he would turn into the ship, but he continued and crashed into the sea."

The pilot house manned as **"General Quarters Battle Stations."**

A young sailor cleaning up after having been rescued from the sea following a battle.

Lt Michael P. Murphy wasn't a tin can sailor, but as a Navy Seal won a Medal of Honor for heroic action in Afghanistan. A new Navy ship, the USS Michael Murphy (DDG-112), an Arleigh Burke class destroyer, has been named after him.

This man's story is told in the book "Lone Survivor" by Marcus Luttrell, and in the movie by the same name.

This is the destroyer class named for Admiral Arleigh Burke, the most famous American destroyer officer of World War 11, and later Chief of Naval Operations.

Experiencing the Kamikaze: "Jap planes were coming at us from all directions."

James J. Fahey joined the Navy in October 1942. He became a Seaman First Class aboard the cruiser USS Montpelier and saw action from the Solomon Islands through the end of the war. On November 27, 1944 the Montpelier was in the Leyte Gulf in support of the American invasion that would eventually liberate the Philippines. The task force that the Montpelier was a part of consisted of 18 ships and this morning they were refueling - the most vulnerable time for an enemy attack.

To protect themselves, the ships formed a defensive circle around the fuel-laden tanker while each took its turn at refueling. If the enemy arrived, sailors armed with axes aboard the refueling warship would cut the fuel lines to allow the ship to get into battle position and as far away from the tanker as possible.

James Fahey kept a diary of his experiences. We join his story as the Montpelier's alarms announce a Japanese attack:

Kamikaze Pilots sit for a portrait before their last flight

"At 10:50 A.M. this morning General Quarters sounded, all hands went to their battle stations. At the same time a battleship and a destroyer were alongside the tanker getting fuel. Out of the clouds I saw a big Jap bomber come crashing down into the water. It was not smoking and looked in good condition. It felt like I was in it as it hit the water not too far from the tanker, and the 2 ships that were refueling. One of our P-38 fighters hit it. He must have got the pilot. At first I thought it was one of our bombers that had engine trouble.

It was not long after that when a force of about 30 Jap planes attacked us. Dive bombers and torpedo planes. Our two ships were busy getting away from the tanker because one bomb-hit on the tanker and it would be all over for the 3 ships.

The 2 ships finally got away from the tanker and joined the circle. I think the destroyers were on the outside of the circle. It looked funny to see the tanker all by itself in the center of the ships as we circled it, with our guns blazing away as the planes tried to break through. It was quite a sight, better than the movies. I never saw it done before. It must be the first time it was ever done in any war.

James J. Fahey, 1943

Jap planes were coming at us from all directions. Before the attack started we did not know that they were suicide planes, with no intention of returning to their base. They had one thing in mind and that was to crash into our ships, bombs and all. You have to blow them up, to damage them doesn't mean much.

Right off the bat a Jap plane made a suicide dive at the cruiser St. Louis there was a big explosion and flames were seen shortly from the stern. Another one tried to do the same thing, but he was shot down. A Jap plane came in on a battleship with its guns blazing away. Other Jap planes came in strafing one ship, dropping their bombs on another and crashing into another ship. The Jap planes were falling all around us, the air was full of Jap machine gun bullets. Jap planes and bombs were hitting all around us. Some of our ships were being hit by suicide planes, bombs and machine gun fire. It was a fight to the finish.

AARON WARD at Kerama Retto, May 1945.

While all this was taking place our ship had its hands full with Jap planes. We knocked our share of planes down, but we also got hit by 3 suicide planes, but lucky for us they dropped their bombs before they crashed into us. In the meantime, exploding planes overhead were showering us with their parts. It looked like it was raining plane parts. They were falling all over the ship. Quite a few of the men were hit by big pieces of Jap planes.

We were supposed to have air coverage but all we had was 4 P-38 fighters, and when we opened up on the Jap planes they got out of the range of our exploding shells. They must have had a ring side seat of the show. The men on my mount were also showered with parts of Jap planes. One suicide dive bomber was heading right for us while we were firing at other attacking planes and if the 40 mm. mount behind us on the port side did not blow the Jap wing off it would have killed all of us. When the wing was blown off it, the plane turned some and bounced off into the water and the bombs blew part of the plane onto our ship.

...A Jap dive bomber crashed into one of the 40 mm. mounts but lucky for them it dropped its bombs on another ship before crashing. Parts of the plane flew everywhere when it crashed into the mount. Part of the motor hit Tomlinson, he had chunks of it all over him, his stomach, back, legs etc. The rest of the crew were wounded, most of them were sprayed with gasoline from the plane. Tomlinson was thrown a great distance and at first they thought he was knocked over the side. They finally found him in a corner in bad shape.

...Planes were falling all around us, bombs were coming too close for comfort. The Jap planes were cutting up the water with machine gun fire. All the guns on the ships were blazing away, talk about action, never a dull moment. The fellows were passing ammunition like lightning as the guns were turning in all directions spitting out hot steel...The deck near my mount was covered with blood, guts, brains, tongues, scalps, hearts, arms etc. from the Jap pilots. The Jap bodies were blown into all sorts of pieces. I cannot think of everything that happened because too many things were happening at the same time. "

References:
James Fahey's account appears in: Fahey, James, Pacific War Diary 1942-1945 (1963); Inoguichi, R, Nakajma T., and Pineau, R. The Divine Wind: Japan's Kamikaze Force in World War Il (1959).

"Kamikaze Attack, 1944," EyeWitness to History, www.eyewitnesstohistory.com (2005).

And hear voices from the other side

'Wings of Defeat': Kamikaze Stories, Told in Person

Determined to die: Ueshima Takeo stands beside his plane.

"Veteran kamikaze pilot" might sound like a contradiction in terms — kamikaze were, after all, the Japanese warriors trained to crash their planes into Allied targets in World War II. Around 4,000 of them died during the war's last days.

But some kamikaze survived, and several of them have been visiting high schools and colleges around the United States. That has led to unusual scenes: classrooms full of teenagers — black, white, Latino, Asian — all teary-eyed from the experience of meeting elderly men once dedicated to fighting America to the death.

Sixteen-year-old Anika Warner, a student at Springbrook High School in Silver Spring, Md., says she never thought the experiences of kamikaze pilots could suddenly feel so personal.

"As good a teacher as you have, no teacher can explain to you how it feels, " Warner says. "[That] your family won't be with you ...you know you're not going to win the war, and you're dying because your country told you to. "

The former kamikaze on the school's tour are featured in a documentary called Wings of Defeat, which examines the frantic, desperate nationalism that engulfed Japan toward the end of the war. The film makes clear that the kamikaze corpsmen weren't volunteers. Most were drafted as teenagers, barely able to fly.

The kamikaze were told that they were gods, heroes, divinely chosen to save their country. They were beaten and brainwashed. Wings of Defeat includes archival footage of officers exhorting their young charges to die.

Ena Takehiko, one of the men visiting Springbrook, flew two suicide missions; both times his plane crashed into the sea. He still has his funeral portrait — a wrinkly black-and-white photo of a handsome 22-year-old staring down the camera, standing by the cockpit he believed would be his coffin.

Takehiko is 84 now, grandfather-age to the Springbrook students. He speaks to them with one of the Wings of Defeat producers translating.

"You know, at the time the kamikaze strategy was a completely last-ditch resort," Takehiko says. "For every 10 kamikaze planes that took off, nine were shot down by the Americans."

Most of the students say they'd never really thought about kamikaze pilots before. If they had, they shared the thoughts of 18-year-old Vikram Madan.

"I guess my view was that these people were these fanatic people, and this really shows they weren't fanatics, " Madan

says. *"They were human, just like me. They were just doing what they were told to do and doing it for the love of their country."*

This classroom is also where 81-year-old Jack Mock meets 85-year-old Ueshima Takeo. Mock was a seaman on the USS Nashville when a kamikaze attacked it in 1944 and killed more than a hundred people. Ueshima was a kamikaze. "*He did his duty; we did ours,*" Ueshima says. And Mock agrees.

"*You were doing your job,*" Mock says. "*We were doing our job. That's all it was no hate, no nothing. You got us, and we got you.* "

The nightmare of Hiroshima and Nagasaki hangs heavily over the former kamikaze's conversation. Ueshima tells the students that the atomic bombing of those cities erased his will to be a warrior.

The former kamikaze say they never could have imagined that they would live to discuss their legacy with American high-school students one day — nor could they have expected those students' compassion.

Source:

https://www.npr.org/templates/story/story.php?storyId=8962 2063

I again saw under the sun that the race is not to the swift and the battle is not to the warriors, and neither is bread to the wise nor wealth to the discerning nor favor to men of ability; for time and chance overtake them all. Moreover, man does not know his time: like fish caught in a treacherous net and birds trapped in a snare, so the sons of men are ensnared at an evil time when it suddenly falls on them.

Ecclesiastes 9: 11

Collisions: a constant concern

And at times ... well the traffic was just a bit heavy and bad things happened

Collision at sea- the amazing story of the USS Murphy (DD-603)

USS Murphy (DD-603)
- Four battle stars for World War Il Service
- Participated in the Normandy Invasion at Omaha Beach
- Escort for the USS Quincy carrying President Franklin D. Roosevelt to the Malta Conference
- Carried the King of Saudi Arabia to the Yalta Conference

The story of the USS Murphy (DD-603) is a fascinating and multi-faceted one.

The story begins in 1943 as Murphy is escorting a large convoy to the British in their valiant efforts to ward off Nazi Germany's plans for the conquest of all of Europe.

As the story unfolds, Murphy is cut in two just 80 miles from New York in a nighttime collision with a large tanker. The forward part of the ship sinks in minutes taking 35 sailors with it, while the stern section is sealed off and towed back to the Brooklyn Navy Yard where it is fitted with a new forward section and sent back into the war effort ... the sort-of-new new ship retains the name Murphy with hull number 603.

The new Murphy continued convoy duty to England; Ireland; Oran, Algeria; Valetta; Malta; Trinidad; and other ports and participated in the invasions of Normandy and Southern France.

In February 1945, the Murphy escorted the Cruiser USS Quincy (CA-71), carrying President Franklin D. Roosevelt and party, across the Atlantic, through Gibraltar and Mediterranean Sea to Oran, Algeria and Malta where FDR departed for the Yalta conference. The Murphy was then dispatched to pick up the King of Saudi Arabia, King Ibn Saud, and his party. Murphy transported the King and his entourage back to Egypt, where King Saud and President Roosevelt had their conference, mainly about the Saudi oil business.

Fast forward to 2000 and the bow of Murphy is discovered by underwater explorer Dan Crowell and his crew aboard the vessel Seeker. Finding the bow of Murphy does not end the story, as Murphy survivors and those left behind, as well as Mr. Crowell endeavor to keep the story alive in the lore of American Naval history.

Some very good coverage of the USS Murphy can be found at these web sites, and I encourage you to take a look.

- Military Channel Quest for Sunken Warships

- USS Murphy Discovery & History
  (http://www.ussmurphydd603.com/Movies.html)

- *USS Murphy DD-603 Association web site
  (http://www.ussmurphydd603.com/index.html)

- Discovery of the USS Murphy (DD-603) and recreation of the collision
  http://wwiv.deepexplorers.com/deep-explorers-tv/questfor-sunken-warships/

- Dan Crowell's web site
  (http://www.dancrowell.com/

The story on the following pages are told by Fred Sheller, one of the survivors of the bow section of the Murphy. I can well relate to this story because my duty stations were those same spaces Fred describes and as you will read later, my ship, the USS Shields (DD-596) came perilously close to a similar collision.

Recollections of the Collision of USS Murphy (DD-603)

By Fredric E. Sheller, former Yeoman 2C, USNR

This states my recollections of the collision occurring between the Destroyer USS Murphy and the American Tanker SS Bulkoil on October 21, 1943, at about 9:20 PM (2120 Hrs. military time), approximately 100 miles out of New York Harbor, as the Murphy and other ships were underway, forming a convoy heading for England.

I had reported aboard the destroyer, USS Murphy, August 28, 1943, as a Seaman Second Class—S2C, for a short time, I was assigned to the First Division (Deck Hand) with BM2C Tom Hilliard as our leader. I then was assigned to be a Striker (OJT) as a Fire Control man in the CIC Room, across from the Ship's Office. I began slowly learning the "ropes" of adjusting to being at sea and receiving training in the Fire Control Field (radar directed aiming of the 5"/38 guns). YIC Duke Mayzurkiewicz (now May-zurk) attempted to get me into the Ship's Office to "strike" for Yeoman, as he was short-handed and needed my help. I declined and was content in staying where I was.

On the night of October 21st, 1943, I was on duty in the CIC Room, along with FCIC or Chief Suellwold (quite certain that's who it was). I had headphones on and was reading training material in the Fire Control man field. Suellwold (again, I believe that's who it was) was back behind the first "computer" (or whatever it was called at that time).

All of a sudden, a call came from, I believe, the Bridge asking for information as to a possible target. I immediately turned the phones over to Suellwold. He began cranking in "stuff" to the computer and I was not aware of what was going on. Suddenly, there was this loud crashing sound, like a Greyhound Bus slamming through large plates of glass.

The lights went out and the emergency wall lantern came on. Seawater began coming into the compartment. Suellwold said, "We'd better get out of here." As I headed for the door, the ship began rolling onto its starboard side. I was grabbing for my lifebelt which was hanging on a hook near the doorway to the compartment. As I attempted to get my lifebelt, I had to grab hold of the doorway frames as the ship continued rolling on its side. The electrical boards in the CIC Room began to topple over. Typewriters and other items began falling through the CIC Room doorway, coming from the Ship's Office, as I was hanging there in midair. I had the feeling that someone fell past me also, but I had no idea who it was.

I lifted myself up onto the bulkhead wall—the ship being completely over by that time—seconds, (I guess) and began crawling along. I suppose, not being totally familiar with the layout of the ship, and especially since it was on its side, and the fact that everything was now covered with crude oil, I slipped down across the next compartment (which was our chow room; men bunked there also) to the other side and fell into crude oil and saltwater. After a few seconds, someone called out, "Who's down there," and I shouted, "Sheller." immediately, someone had me by the belt and seat of my dungarees and pulled me up out of there (I never found out who that was). Several other shipmates and I began climbing the Galley way double-ladder (stairs). The bow now on its side; in the dark, of course, except for a lighted emergency lantern (which automatically came on when the electrical lights went out) hanging on the bulkhead. We got almost to the top of the ladder, it being on its side, and a couple shipmates up above, in the Galley way, closed and began "dogging" the double-hatch watertight cover (proper shipwreck procedures in order to attempt to save the ship or to keep it afloat longer) thereby trapping us down below. Someone grabbed the lighted emergency lantern from the bulkhead (unknown* at the time who it was, but identified below) and he started heading forward, calling out "Follow me," with a couple of shipmates* and me following, crawling on our hands and knees, through upturned equipment, bunks, debris, etc. All we could do was head to higher levels as the ship was sinking fast. Seems we headed for where we smelled fresh air. I can't tell exactly where we came out from below the main focsle deck, but I have always believed that it was Gun Mount #2. Whoever was in front of me getting through the mess below deck had already gotten up to the side lifeline, slipped into the water as the ship was sinking, or were somewhere else. I had no way of knowing about them. I had to try to get off the bow somehow. (* These shipmates possibly were Yeoman rkiewicz and Pharmacist Mate Trotter.)

> (*Reference the asterisk in the preceding paragraph. After many years and with the discovery of that part of the ship which sank (covered below), I have found who these shipmates were. My comments regarding the discovery and these shipmates is covered towards the end of this written account.)

As I stood up on the slanted Gun Mount #2, I looked down to my left and could see the phosphorescence bubbles of seawater enveloping the bow as it was going down. I was slipping around as my shoes were so oily from the crude oil. There was no way that I was going to get out of my predicament, so I sat down on the gun mount, took off my shoes and socks, and because I couldn't get my belt-buckle to open (didn't have my Navy knife attached to my belt where I could cut the belt), I rolled up my dungaree pants legs to high on my legs, ripped off my shirt. I was then ready to "dig in" and jump up to catch the lifeline on the side of the bow. I knew that I had to make that jump the first time! I was a short sailor at only 5'5" and that was a long jump! I pulled myself up onto the side of the bow and could see two or three persons at the forward edge of the bow near the port anchor. When I got to them, I saw that it was our Skipper, Commander Bailey; the others I didn't recognize. The

Skipper had a light of some sort. He finally said, "Well, boys. Looks like we'll have to get off here." And then, I jumped into the water (it was high in the air and I couldn't estimate that height). I just knew that I had to get off there in a hurry!

Remembering my basic (boot) training at Sampson Naval Training Station, New York, as soon as I hit the water, I began to swim for all I was worth as I could feel the pull (like suction) of the bow going down. After a while, I turned onto my back, looked back at the bow still up high in the air. Our Skipper was still there apparently because I could see a light. I don't know how he got off the bow. Phosphorous was hitting me as I struggled in the water, swimming, floating, praying (not for me, but for my family and friends). That phosphorous hitting me was a burning sensation. It was still pitch black and the sea was quite choppy. I could see the fluorescent phosphorous in the waves. I kept swimming and floating with no way of knowing at the time if I would be rescued. I heard yelling and shouting in the immediate distance, so I started swimming towards those sounds. I then could see that a ship was out there with searchlights playing over the water, and the lights never stopping in one place. They kept moving! It was a weird feeling, as though they weren't seeing anyone in the water, but I could see heads bobbing around. I thought to myself, "My God they don't see us!"

All of a sudden something hit me, and I recognized it as a small fresh water cask (evidently it came out of one of the life rafts). I grabbed hold of both ends of it with my fingers and held on. I wasn't able to get it under my arm. I kept hold of that cask, paddling with my feet towards the sounds that I had heard. Then, I came upon a life raft with shipmates in the middle of it and others holding on to ropes all around the outboard of the raft. Suddenly, someone, holding on to the raft, grabbed my right wrist, held onto me and I finally lost the cask. But, I was fortunate that someone got hold of me and I was safe alongside the raft. I discovered later that it was Emmet S. Wold, CSK (Chief Storekeeper).

The raft drifted alongside the ship rescuing us (the USS Glennon DD620). While the raft kept banging against the side of the rescue ship, I'm sure that we lost some shipmates right there as they were being slammed against the ship due to the heavy waves. I saw that some of the crew of the rescue ship was tossing ropes down to us. I finally grabbed hold of one, but the rope kept slipping through my extremely cold and oily hands as the guys on the ship were pulling up the rope. However, luckily there was a huge knot towards the end of the rope, and when my closed hands got to this knot, up I went to the deck of the ship where Glennon crew members were awaiting to assist me.

I didn't observe any of the other rescue efforts done by the crew of the USS Glennon as I was immediately taken into the head (bathroom to non-sailors) where diesel oil was applied all over me by Glennon crew members in order to get the black, crude (fuel) oil off. After this was done, I was put in a cold shower, and then a hot shower to get me cleaned up. I presumed that other shipmates of mine who were rescued were given the same treatments. Then I was given a good shot of whiskey in order to get my heart and body back to normal temperature and to relieve the shock. Next, I was taken below deck to the crew sleeping quarters and was given a bunk to sleep in with extra, navy blankets to get me warmed up. I must have fallen asleep right away because next thing I remember is next morning when I was given some clothing by Glennon crew members. A tall, black mess steward gave me his set of whites. I had to roll up the sleeves and pants legs as they were so long. It was a kind gesture for him to give me his clothing and I thanked him, never knowing if I would ever be able to see him again and return his clothing. In fact, I never did! Someone gave me a pair of heavy, woolen socks which I used as shoes the next few days.

That was my dress outfit for the next few days. Even when we survivors were transferred to other ships, transported to pier 92 in New York and while being processed there by the Navy, I wore the same outfit until proper clothing was issued. Ships transporting rescued back to New York were the USCGC Cartigan, which I was on, and the PYC 37. I was transferred to the USCGC Cartigan just after noontime on October 22, 1943, one of 100 officers and crewmen that ship received.

The Glennon passed a towline to the after section of the Murphy, still afloat, and began towing it just after midnight of 21-22 October 1943. At about 1153 hours, October 22, 1943, the civilian tug SS Rescue took over towing the Murphy from the Glennon, heading back to the Brooklyn Navy Yard, N.Y.

Repairs began immediately on the Murphy, to get a new bow section constructed (half the ship actually). Crew members were assigned to quarters on Myrtle Avenue, Brooklyn, while this reconstruction was taking place. Quite a few men were transferred to other ships, schools and various assignments.

I was asked by YIC Mayzurkiewicz (Mayzurk) to help him establish an office on the dock where I could help him with reports, reconstructing lost records of the officers and crew, and other administrative duties. I accepted this request from Duke and began these duties with him and our New Executive Officer, Lt. J. A McTighe. Since there was no work for me to do on the ship otherwise, I volunteered to help. After a short time, Mayzurk managed to get me promoted to Seaman 1C. Mayzurk eventually had to be transferred to the hospital due to some injuries he received in the collision. Mr. McTighe had his wife come into the office to help with our administrative operations. She helped me tremendously in getting adjusted to Admin work. Then, Yeoman IC Tim Barrett came aboard and we worked together in the office. Barrett got me to be interested in becoming a Yeoman, had me complete the Yeoman Third Class course, and finally got me promoted to Yeoman 3C.

I had so much running around to do, getting mail and reports delivered to proper offices at the Navy Yard and Post Office that Mr. McTighe managed to get me a bicycle for use in getting my running done. I kept the bicycle on the ship when we were recommissioned and out to sea a few months later. The bicycle was then used by me and the other yeomen as well as the ship's mailman when we got back into a port.

The Casualties Folder for the Murphy at the National Archives includes a list of 38 officers and men declared missing, but a later memorandum states that 3 of those listed were rescued by the USS Jeffers (DD621), an escort ship which was part of the forming convoy. Finally, in April 1944, the Murphy, with a new forward section, was ready for sea once again. The ship participated in many convoy escort duties crossing the Atlantic Ocean to England; Ireland; Oran, Algeria; Valetta; Malta; Trinidad; and other ports, and participated in the invasions of Normandy and Southern France. In February 1945, the Murphy escorted the Cruiser USS Quincy (CA-71), carrying President Franklin D. Roosevelt and party, across the Atlantic, through Gibraltar and Mediterranean Sea to Oran, Algeria and Malta where FDR departed for the Yalta conference. The Murphy was then dispatched through the Suez Canal and Red Sea to Jidda Arabia to pick up the King of Saudi Arabia, King Ibn Saud, and his party of 48 personnel. The King's provisions included rugs, pots and pans for cooking, rice, sheep for slaughter, furniture and tent material. The King originally had intended to feed the entire crew but was persuaded to bring aboard just enough food items for his own party. We transported the King and his entourage back up the Red Sea to Great Bitter Lake, Egypt, where we tied up alongside the Cruiser Quincy and King Saud and President Roosevelt had their conference, mainly about the Saudi oil business.

Following this voyage, the Murphy steamed through the Panama Canal to San Diego en-route to the far East Okinawa, Eniwetok, Nagasaki, Japan, (September 22-23, 1945- where one atomic bomb had been dropped in August 1945). The ship subsequently visited ports of Wakayama, Nagoya and Yokosuka.

On October 16'th 2002, I received an email from Captain Dan Crowell, undersea diver based in New Jersey, who reported that he and his diving crew, aboard his diving vessel SEEKER, had discovered, in the summer of 2000, long-lost vessel 80 miles off the New Jersey coast in 200+ feet of seawater. That discovery subsequently proved to be the remains of the USS Murphy. I immediately responded with an email to Captain Crowell and we and the remaining Murphy crew began a deep friendship which continues to the current time. Captain Crowell has interviewed me and many of the Murphy crew in an effort to publish a documentary about the Murphy saga. Captain Dan and his wife Jenifer, affectionately referred to as "Jenn, " attend as many of the Murphy reunions as they possibly can and are considered to be part of the Murphy Family. This discovery has brought back many memories from the past! In many emails and phone conversations, I have found that the shipmate who guided me and possibly two other shipmates up out of the sinking forward section of the Murphy, following the collision between the tanker SS Bulkoil on October 21, 1943, the shipmate mentioned at the beginning of this document, was Gunner's Mate 3c Raymond C. Preeshl. After many discussions together of our facts and thoughts, both Ray and I know that he was the shipmate carrying that emergency lantern, leading us out of the ship. He was the shipmate who saved our lives that night!

Preeschl always took stock of where he was and when first reporting aboard the ship, or any ship, studied the various routes to exit himself from various compartments of the ship. Preeschl states that we came out of Gun Mount #2, first through the men's forward "Head," then through the Ammo Handling Room below the gun mount. I definitely remember exiting the door of the Gun Mount and readying myself for jumping up to the port lifeline.

Through many discussions between Ray and myself, and other shipmates, we have determined that the two possible shipmates who were between me and Preeschl were YIC Duke Mayzurk and PhM2C Trottier.

On September 16th, 2004, the USS Murphy Sailors Organization dedicated a Memorial Monument to our thirty-five lost shipmates at the Veteran's Park, Surf City (Long Island), New Jersey.

The documentary which Captain Dan Crowell has been working on has "aired" over New York TV Channel 7 and has been "aired" several times on the TV History Channel program "Deep Sea Detectives," with the title, "Destroyer Down." In addition, I was interviewed by Reporter Dan Adams, of KYIV Channel 10 News, Sacramento, CA, relating my experiences, and this program was also aired" several times locally. Captain Crowell has made a DVD of his documentary which includes his interviews with me and many of my shipmates.

Fred Sheller speaking at the dedication of the USS Murphy Memorial in Veterans Memorial Park Surf City, New Jersey. September 2004

USS Murphy (DD-603)

Murphy - severely stricken, but back in action in short order with a new bow section and an amazing future

Survivors remember their shipmates

USS Frank E. Evans (DD-754)

Ohhh ... my goodness, is that a tin can about to be cut in two?

USS Frank E. Evans (DD-754)

Honors and awards:
1 battle star (World War II)
5 battle stars (Korean War)

HMS Melbourne

The USS Frank E. Evans (DD-754) somehow found itself directly in the path of the Australian aircraft carrier Melbourne.

At around 3 a.m. on 3 June 1969, between Vietnam and Spratly Island, Evans was operating with the Royal Australian Navy in company with Melbourne which was at flying stations. Melbourne signaled Evans, then to port of the carrier, to take up the rescue destroyer position.

The logical movement would be to turn to port and describe a circle taking up station on the carrier's port quarter. Inexplicably, instead of turning to port, Evans turned to starboard, cutting across Melbourne's bow, and was cut in half in the ensuing collision. She crossed the bow of the Melbourne twice as she was hit on the port side. Her bow drifted off to the Melbourne's port side and sank after about ten to twenty minutes taking 74 of her crew with it. The stern scraped along the starboard side of the Melbourne and lines were able to be attached by the Melbourne's crew. Around another 60-100 men were rescued from the water. At the time of the collision Evans's captain was asleep. The officer of the deck (a junior officer who was not qualified to stand watch, having failed at his previous board) failed to notify him when he executed the station change, as required by the Commanding Officer's standing orders.

Source: http://en.wikipedia.org/wiki/USS_Frank_E._Evans_ (DD-754)

My own sea story - Collision at Sea

This is a story from after my active duty Porterfield days and I was assigned to the reserve ship USS Shields (DD-596) to finish up four more years of reserve duty. We were steaming North past San Francisco and taking on fuel. My job was to help haul over the fueling lines from the oiler. Once pulled over, my job was done, and I was off to my rack for a few Z's. After just dozing off, I was rudely awakened by the clanging collision alarm. I quickly jumped out of the rack and bounded up the ladder to the forward hatch in the bow to see what was going on. By then the ship was shuddering under a full power reversal. I looked to my right and there coming out of a patchy fog bank was a large freighter steaming right across the path of our three-ship refueling formation; us on the starboard of the oiler and another destroyer, the USS Agerholm, on the port side. The Agerholm had broken away from the oiler and was breaking hard to port at flank speed in order to clear the area. The Oiler could only try to back down but because of its huge mass and lack of maneuvering room was essentially helpless. We were, for a time, trapped between the oiler and the freighter, eventually backing clear of the oncoming freighter. After what seemed an eternity, the two ships collided with the oiler hitting the freighter just below the bridge, causing it to list at about 40 some degrees. Eventually it righted itself, but there was a huge gaping hole in the hull. Fortunately, the seas were calm, the freighter was riding high in the water and the bow of the oiler hit well above the water line. The ship did not sink.

In spite of events such as this, I enjoyed being at sea. There is just something majestic in experiencing the huge overpowering waves and the still of the night on a calm sea watching the luminescent wake under a sky full of stars.

When you pass through the waters, I will be with you;
And through the rivers, they shall not overflow you.
When you walk through the fire, you shall not be burned,
Nor shall the flame scorch you.

Isaiah 43:2

Sr. Chief Rob O'Neill -A hometown hero

The Man Who Killed Osama Bin Laden Rob O'Neill and I were both raised in Butte Montana, and both of us joined the US Navy at age 19. Rob stayed with the Navy for 17 some years and had quite a remarkable career. If you haven't seen his interview with Peter Doocy on Fox News I encourage you to watch it at

https://www.youtube.com/watch?v=W6YpWSfZ150 & https://www.youtube.com/watch?v=4UTijlIKa7U

Going public has caused a bit of controversy over whether the former Seal is "cashing in" on his role in killing bin Laden, but I will let Rob's words at the 33:54 mark of Part 2 in the interview stand as the answer ... I personally support his going public for the reasons he states.

During his military career, he was awarded with 52 medals, including two Silver Stars, three Presidential Unit citations and four Bronze Stars for valor.

I Didn't Want to Worry You Dad ...

Though I titled this book "I Didn't Want to Worry You Mom ... ", I actually compiled the book with a much larger audience in mind as seen in the introductory pages of the book.

At about the 31:30 mark of the interview, O'Neill recounts the phone call he made to his father just prior to the team's departure to Pakistan. This phone call, the last Rob would make before the mission, carries a tone of finality ... a goodbye to his father, and a tone which his father picked up on in that final conversation.

Here is a warrior ... a warrior off again on a very dangerous and secretive mission ... a mission in which he doesn't "want to worry you Mom ... and Dad", but one in which he can't disclose anything.

As you will see in the following pages, this man O'Neill, like many with him, before him, and those that will follow set off on dangerous missions in which the outcome was high risk and very uncertain.

The US Navy Rescue of Captain Richard Phillips

On April 8, the destroyer USS Bainbridge (DDG-96) and the frigate USS Halyburton (FFG-40) were dispatched to the Gulf of Aden in response to a hostage situation and reached Maersk Alabama early on April 9. Maersk Alabama then departed from the area with an armed escort towards its original destination of the port of Mombasa. On Saturday, April 11, Maersk Alabama arrived in Mombasa, still under U.S. military escort. Captain Larry Aasheim then assumed command. Aasheim had previously been captain of the Maersk Alabama until Richard Phillips relieved him eight days prior to the pirate attack. An 18-man marine security team was on board. The U.S. Federal Bureau of Investigation secured the ship as a crime scene.

On April 9, a standoff began between the Bainbridge and the pirates in the Maersk Alabama 's lifeboat where they continued to hold Phillips hostage. Three days later, U.S. Navy marksmen from DEVGRU (formerly known as SEAL

Team Six) opened fire and killed the three pirates on the lifeboat, and Phillips was rescued in good condition. The Bainbridge captain, Commander Frank Caste, ordered the action after determining that Phillips' life was in immediate danger based on reports that a pirate was pointing an AK-47 automatic rifle at his back. Navy SEAL snipers on Bainbridge's fantail opened fire, killing the three pirates with bullets to the head.

A fourth pirate, aboard the Bainbridge and speaking with military negotiators while being treated for an injury sustained in the takeover of Maersk Alabama, surrendered and was taken into custody. He later pleaded guilty to hijacking, kidnapping and hostage-taking charges and was sentenced to over 33 years in prison.

This hostage/pirate episode was the basis for the movie "Captain Phillips. "

It has been subsequently disclosed that the leader of SEAL Team Six was Sr. Chief Rob O'Neill.

Navy SEALs -Operation Redwing

United States Navy file photo of Navy SEALs operating in Afghanistan in support of Operation Enduring Freedom. From left to right, Sonar Technician (Surface) 2nd Class Matthew G. Axelson, of Cupertino, Calif; Senior Chief Information Systems Technician Daniel R. Healy, of Exeter, N.H.; Quartermaster 2nd Class James Suh, of Deerfield Beach, Fla.; Hospital Corpsman 2nd Class Marcus Luttrell; Machinist's Mate 2nd Class Eric S. Patton, of Boulder City, Nev.; and Lt. Michael P. Murphy, of Patchogue, N.Y. With the exception of Luttrell, all were killed June 28, 2005, by enemy forces while supporting Operation Redwing.

Under the cover of night, a 4-man SEAL team was inserted high up in the Afghan mountains. The team consisted of 3 petty officers, Matthew Axelson, Danny Dietz and Marcus Luttrell and was led by Lt. Michael P. Murphy. The SEALs had been on a number of previous operations in the Hindu

Kush mountains. Taliban and Al Qaeda forces regularly sought refuge in these almost impassible mountain ranges and the SEALs had been sent in to hunt them down.

Sometime after sun up, the SEALs were discovered by a small group of goat herders who had walked right into the Observation Point. The SEALs were now faced with a dilemma: do they execute the goat herders or let them go? In a decision that would haunt the mission's sole survivor, the SEALs decided to let the goat herders go, knowing full well there was a good chance they would alert local Taliban forces to the SEAL's presence on the mountain.

In an attempt to stay ahead of the Taliban, the SEALs switched to an alternate Observation Point and resumed their mission. A few hours later, they were approached by a large force of Taliban fighters. Surrounded left, right and forward, with a sheer drop down the mountainside behind them, the SEALs had no option but to try and fight their way out and so they opened fire.

A fierce and prolonged firefight ensued. The SEALs were unable to raise their HQ on their radio so were unable to call for backup. With more Taliban coming at them, the SEALs made a series of fighting withdrawals, moving down the dangerously steep mountain walls, pursued all the while by the relentless Taliban fighters.

All but one SEAL was unwounded by Taliban gunfire. Their situation was getting desperate. They still had no comms with their base and the Taliban kept on coming, no matter how many they felled. In a selfless act, the team leader, Lt. Michael P. Murphy, took out his cell phone and moved out into the open in order to get a connection to the HQ. Exposed, Murphy was gunned down by the Taliban but not before he was able to send out a brief distress call.

Forced to retreat further still, disaster again hit the SEALs as petty officers Matthew Axelson and Danny Dietz were both killed in action. The sole surviving SEAL, petty officer Marcus Luttrell fended off his pursuers while trying to get to safety.

Meanwhile, a rescue force of SEALs had loaded into a MH-47 Chinook helicopter and were now flying into the area in a bid to rescue their brothers. Unfortunately, the Taliban were ready for them and as the huge helicopter came into a hover over the SEAL's planned insertion point, an RPG was fired straight through the Chinook's open rear ramp. The rocket struck the internal fuel tanks and the helicopter exploded and crashed in a ball of flame. 8 SEALs and 8 Night Stalkers were killed. The only upside of this tragedy was that it had diverted many of the Taliban pursuing the original SEAL team away to engage it.

Elsewhere in this book I point out the honor bestowed on Lt. Michael P. Murphy beyond his Medal of Honor, that honor of having an Arleigh Burke class destroyer named in his honor.

Sr. Chief Rob O'Neill led a subsequent mission that rescued Marcus Luttrell. The story of Luttrell and the battle in those high mountains turned into the 2013 movie "Lone Survivor." "He is still friendly with Marcus, they had dinner together just the other day, " said O'Neill's father.

<u>Editorial Note;</u> This from SEAL Adm. Brian Insey: "Our Ethos is a life-long commitment and obligation, both in and out of the Service. Violators of our Ethos are neither Teammates in good standing, nor Teammates who represent Naval Special Warfare We do not abide willful or selfish disregard for our core values in return for public notoriety and financial gain."

I understand and respect this Ethos, but I also believe that in such an Ethos, room must be made for exceptions - exceptions based on exceptional circumstances. The exceptional circumstance in O'Neill's case was the September 2001 attack on 2,996 innocent civilians on American soil. O'Neill's encounter in the New York Ground Zero museum with family members Of 9/11 victims convinces me that O'Neill did not violate the SFAL Ethos. On the contrary, he upheld it in the highest possible way given the exceptional circumstance of 9/11/2001.

A hometown and national hero

This is why Rob O'Neill was there.

Butte has long had a reputation as a tough mining town and having grown up there myself I can attest to that ... although not on a personal level. I knew some pretty tough characters there, and some who would fight at the drop of a hat.

But Rob O'Neill shows a toughness that goes well beyond ... a toughness of continual service to his country. Toughness we can all be grateful for in a man living at the tip of the spear of liberty.

Butte: A Mile High and a Mile Deep

Rob O'Neill went half way around the world to stare evil in the face.

*Freedom was attacked -
and America responded...*

That will be the legacy of the man who killed Osama Bin Laden

You and I have a rendezvous with destiny. We will preserve for our children this, the last best hope of man on earth, or we will sentence them to take the first step into a thousand years of darkness. If we fail, at least let our children and our children's children say of us we justified our brief moment here. We did all that could be done.

Ronald Reagan

Off Duty - Liberty Call

An old friend - John (Jack) Hix

Ann Margaret on USO tour

Kaohsiung, a liberty port on the island of Taiwan

Home again once more!

Liberty Call at long last! Do you recognize Senator John McCain prisoner of war for 6 years?

And what of those tin can sailors?

Gene Beckstrom - Jack Spradlin - Sam Thomas - Warren Seward

Shipmates from World War II

I grew up watching the television series "Victory at Sea" on our old black and white TV. But those scenes from World War Il seemed so distant from me ... a different time far removed from a teenager in Butte Montana who had never even seen an ocean.

I joined the Navy in 1964 and served on one of those old "tin cans" I'd heard about and read about and seen on those old videos ... but that war and those sailors still seemed so distant in time and geography from a young man of 20.

Then in 2013 my wife Diana and I attended our first USS Balch-Porterfield reunion where I actually met these heroes ... men who have been called the "Greatest Generation" ... men who saved the world.

There I was among them, talking with them and breaking bread with them and hearing them call me "shipmate." I was honored and humbled to be with them and learn of their lives, both as sailors, and in their subsequent civilian life. Some of the wives of those sailors were also there. We learned of their stories as well.

So a circle was closed for me. I now count as dear friends – comrades in arms – fellow shipmates, those same sailors I watched on that black & white TV in Butte Montana.

Warren and Sam served on the Balch in the Pacific war. Balch earned six battle stars, including the decisive Battle of Midway in which she rescued 545 survivors of the carrier Yorktown.

Gene, Jack and Sam served on the Porterfield during the Pacific war. Porterfield received nine battle stars for World War Il, and four more for Korea. Gene served six years in the Navy and later served twenty years in the Army including combat service with the 25'th Division in the Korean War.

Tom Hamilton - Larry Wieland - Tom Page - Pat Fisher

Shipmates from the Korean War and the Cold War

<u>Front row:</u> Van Hardesty ... Mike Casillas ... Richard Gomez ... John Bryan ... David Lesh
<u>Back row:</u> Don Godfrey ... Jack Corcoran ... Bill Harris ... Don Johnson

Shipmates from the Vietnam War

Our Skipper - Cdr James R. Switzer on the 1966 Porterfield deployment to Vietnam

A graduate of the US Merchant Marine Academy, the skipper spent 30 years in the US Navy where he had numerous duty assignments, retiring in 1980. He served during the Korean and Vietnam Wars and was stationed for many years in California. He worked for a time at the Pentagon, was with the Diplomatic Corps in Santiago, Chile as the Naval Attaché/Defense Attaché, and in Charleston, SC with the Naval Investigative Service. Captain Switzer served on numerous ships and three destroyers, including commanding the minesweeper the USS Fortify and the USS Porterfield.

Our Executive Officer (XO) - Lcdr Paul D. Butcher on the 1966 Porterfield deployment to Vietnam

Admiral Butcher joined the Navy as an apprentice seaman in 1948. He was commissioned an ensign five years later and rose to a destroyer command during the Vietnam War. He was the first director of planning of the Rapid Deployment Joint Task Force, which drew up detailed plans for protecting Persian Gulf oilfields.
During the 1991 war against Iraq, he served as chief of staff and deputy commander of the United States Transportation Command.

Admiral Butcher, an avid baseball fan and friend of George Steinbrenner, the principal owner of the New York Yankees, retired in 1991. Mr. Steinbrenner named him his successor as chairman and chief executive of the American Ship Building Company in Tampa, Fla. Admiral Butcher was head of the company at his death.

Pastoral Perspective

I have just completed one of the most enjoyable trips of my life, "The Veterans Honor Flight." The reception that we received from the people at the airport in Duluth Minnesota, and the people in Washington D.C. was overwhelming.

At 4 am when I arrived at the Duluth airport the ticket area was jammed-packed with people and everyone wanted to say, "Thank you for your service" and the same at the airport in Washington D.C. There was 60 veterans and 60 guardians that pushed us all in wheelchairs over the entire day. When we arrived back in Duluth at 11:45 pm, the arrival area was again jam packed with people that welcomed us back to Duluth.

My "Guardian" was Dr. David Mast who is a doctor at St. Lukes hospital in Duluth. Not only did he push me in a wheel chair all day, but he took my camera and took over 200 pictures of some of the areas we visited in Washington. The picture here is of Senator Dole who was at one of our stops and he talked with us and had his picture taken with a few of the veterans.

Gene Beckstrom

A Young Bride Left Behind

What of those loved ones left behind?

- A mother or father left behind ...
- A grandmother or grandfather left behind ...
- A wife left behind ...
- A son or daughter or a grandchild who wonders...
- what did dad or grandpa do during the war?
- what was it like?
- A brother or sister left behind ...
- A good friend left behind ...

My cousin Reidun was such a young bride in 1968. An immigrant from Norway, she fell in love with a young man of Norwegian heritage and they were married in Seattle.

I'll let Reidun's words represent the anguish that many of those left behind over the centuries and around the world as their loved ones went off to war.

Read the words to follow and hear in your own heart and soul the anguish war brings.

Fall of 1968

After Fort Ord he was sent back home to Fort Lewis until he was shipped off to Vietnam on December 16, 1968.
We got married August 3, 1968.
His orders came in October 1968.
The most horrible shock of my life thus far.

I had never felt such fear and anger grip my heart before.
Such strong emotions frightened me even more than the news of being sent off to the war.
I had never felt anger at the Lord before, that terrified me.
I ran into our bedroom, knelt by a chair grabbing a tight hold of that chair, I cried out to the Lord:

Lord, please take this hard, cold anger away from me.
I do not want to be angry with you, Please Lord, your will be done, but please Lord, give me a Word to trust in.
Will he come back home in one piece safely to me?
As I prayed my heart quieted down.

The Lord said:
As the Lions did not eat Daniel, and as the three friends did not burn in the fire, so it will be with Kjell also.
He will be returned to you safely, not a hair of his head will be touched.

I arose, I had peace, I had a Word and a promise from the Lord.

Poor Kjell. They lined all soldiers going to Vietnam up like sheep to slaughter. A long line -- as they went through they were given various immunization shots in both arms.
He came home sore and swollen in both arms.
Next two of his wisdom teeth were pulled out, bits of jaw bone to go with that.

He bled all over the pillow at night, the young man was in pain.
But worst was the strange emotional change that came over him.
Outwardly to others he seemed like the same guy, but he put on a protective mode for himself to cover up for the fear that he felt as well.

Our honey moon days ended that October 1968, he was different now.

I was already beginning to feel like a war window, with the prospect of being left in the States without him, the only reason I still remained in the US.
Although for the grace of God I still had Joanne and Bob living in Seattle, and all the Harjo family.
When he left for Vietnam I moved in with his parents, but it felt as my reason for living was gone.
Now it became a year of survival mode for both of us, he in the war, I at home praying day and night for his protection, as did our parents, our family and our church and friends.

It was the Vietnam Tet offensive, intense fighting.
I have newspaper clipping from the action.
He arrived in Saigon right before Christmas of 1968, In the 25th infantry division.
He was put to work in the morgue upon arrival, sorting the living from the dead, body parts from body parts.
The helicopters would come in with the wounded and the dead, he was there to help unload and sort the living from the dead.

Soon after he arrived his officer got too close to the swiftly moving helicopter blades, part of his scalp was cut off.
Kjell jumped on him thus the officer was not decapitated.

Kjell earned a bronze star right off the bat for saving an officer's life.

As a chaplain assistant he had to drive the chaplain in their jeep to the front lines and assist in all services.
They were shot at and bombed at and blown out of their bunks at night.

One day as lunch was about to be served out on the front lines, the chaplain said: Let's go and get our chow.
They no sooner left that spot than then an incoming mortar hit the spot exactly where they had been standing.

Time and again his life was thus spared.

Time and again I woke up at night hit the floor and prayed, because Kjell's life was in danger.
Even if you have a Word and a promise from the Lord you still have to obey that word and pray it through.

He slept alone in fox holes out on the front lines.
One night he wrote to me by a small light in such a hole: The only company I have is a small frog.

He was a man of prayer and worship and the Word.
He did not use alcohol and drugs.

He had the Lord.

Though I walk in the valley of the Shadow of death I will fear no evil.

Kjell came home from the war -- alive with *not a hair of his head touched.*

And the Lord prospered him and Reidun in many ways.

THE LITTLE WIFE I LEFT BEHIND

As I lay down and dream tonight,
    And the past comes to my mind,
I think of someone lovely
    It's the little wife I left behind.

If I could only be with you tonight
    And take you in my arms,
Or hold you on my knee once more
    And view your lovely charms.

Darling, I never knew until I was away
    How sweet and precious you could be.
You're just a lovely thing from Heaven,
    And you mean more than life to me.

When I was home and with you, dear,
    You, so lovely, sweet and kind,
I never dreamed I'd miss you so
    When I left you there behind.

But I know your brave as you carry on,
    And I know you'll do your part
To keep our home or build us planes
    And guns, God bless your heart.

And if it wasn't for sweetheart wives,
    What would we be fighting for?
It's for you and other loved ones, dear,
    We Buddies will die or win this war.

So as the moon shines down on the battle field
    And lights up the old Red, White and Blue,
I know the same moon is shining on you there
    And I'll soon be coming back to you.

So Darling, where there's life, there's hope
    As o'er the battle fields we trod,
But Dear, you're fighting a battle too,
    And our hope and destiny is with God.

                                J Frank Astle
                                1379 N. St. Francis
                                Wichita, Kansas.

"Pivot Point"

Military units have call signs. Pilots and aircrews have call signs and handles.

Over the years I worked with Major Marc "Foxy" Foxwell, Mike "Mauler" Gunther, Harry "Snake" Houghton and others.

Navy ships also have call signs, and "Pivot Point" was the call sign for USS Porterfield. Standing many bridge watches on old DD-682, I heard "Pivot Point" crackle over the radio waves on many occasions.

Reuniting with my 1965-66 shipmates of the Porterfield, and meeting others who served on her during WW-II, Korea and the Cold War has for me been a "Pivot Point" in my life.

Sam Thomas

I remember well that first reunion in 2013 when Sam Thomas, a WW-II veteran and founder of the reunion association spoke at the farewell banquet. Sam said *"I'm 90 years old and I don't know how many more of these reunions I will be able to attend. I just want all of you know – no matter what your job, no matter when you served, no matter how long you served – you and I are shipmates and friends."*

Sam attended 40 consecutive reunions and was well loved by all. I count it a high honor to have known him and to hear him call me shipmate and friend, a friend and shipmate who

I first encountered as a teenager on that black & white TV in Butte Montana in the 50s as I watched Victory at Sea.

For my 4th reunion in 2016, I was chosen to host the event in my long-time hometown of San Diego, the home port of so many crews of Porterfield over the years, and a pier where that ship pushed off in the dark of night to war in the South Pacific. Two years, seven months and twenty-four days of continual war-time sea duty, that crew finally came home and became part of that *"Greatest Generation."*

Sam called me several months before the San Diego reunion and told me: *"Don, there is just so much wrong with my body, and I'm afraid I won't be able to make the reunion this year."*

Sam passed in early 2017.

Gene Beckstrom

Again, going back to 2013 and my first reunion. I had recorded the memorial service where those shipmates and spouses who passed in the previous year were honored by a reading of names and the ringing of a ship's bell for each name called out.

After the service, I announced I would post the video on the internet and asked if there were those who did not have internet access. Gene Beckstrom, who served alongside Sam Thomas down in the engine rooms during the battles of the South Pacific was one who requested a CD of the service, so I mailed a copy to him in Minnesota.

Awhile later, while we were vacationing along the coast of Maine, I got a phone call from Gene thanking me for the video. I remember my reaction to that phone call. I was surprised, honored and humbled that this man would call me. I felt inadequate. That phone call began a very close friendship with this man I grew to love and respect so much in the few short years I knew him. We talked at length during the next several reunions as I learned much of this man's life.

To recap a bit of Gene's life:

Gene was a troubled teenager in St. Paul, and a trouble maker. Gene told me that he stole pennies off the tops of milk bottles on the porches of neighbors.

At 16 he was faced with a choice: off to reform school and probably a career in crime and prison - or join the Navy. This was in the midst of World War II, so the choices were stark. The judge took Gene to the Navy recruiting office and told the recruiter *"sign this kid up!"* The recruiter began the process and asked, *"How old are you son?"* to which Gene answered *"16 Sir!"* The judge leaned into the recruiter's face and said, *"He's 18 – now who ya gonna to believe, this lying kid or me a judge? Sign him up!"* Gene joined the Navy that day.

Gene's entry into the Navy was not all that smooth. Early on he went AWOL missed ships movement and wound up in the brig for a few days before the deployment of the Porterfield.

Then and now, the Navy was a place where growing up occurred. Gene experienced this sometimes harsh growing up under the no-nonsense rule of seasoned old salts. Sam Thomas was one of those old salts who slapped this young snot-nosed brat upside the head on occasion.

In these later years, Gene expressed much gratitude to the Navy, and to men like Sam Thomas for turning his life around. And to the extended Navy family left behind on that pier who took Gene's young wife under their wing during those long and tough years of war.

A touching, and somewhat humorous thing happened at our Buffalo reunion in 2014. I had just published the first edition of this book along with a 20-minute companion video. I showed the video to the group, and on the left side of the room was Beckstrom and on the right side was Thomas. After the video there was a bit of sharing back and forth, and Gene looked over at Sam with tears in his eyes telling him how grateful he was that an *"old salt"* like Sam came into his life and transformed it.

The next morning Sam approached me and said *"Don, I was that old salt Gene was talking about and I was only 19 years old!"* Stories such as this highlight the character of that *"greatest generation."*

Gene finished his duty in the Navy in 1946, and then joined the Army. In June 1950 he was stationed in Okinawa. That was when the North Korean Army rolled across the 38th Parallel and drove the South Korean defenders to a small corner of the peninsula call the Pusan Perimeter. Gene's unit was the first American unit called to Korea, and Gene spent the next several years, to 1953, as a combat engineer fighting the North Koreans and Chinese armies up and down the Korean peninsula.

Combat was tough and brutal, and the ground forces received Naval Gun Fire Support from ships off shore. Gene recalls one such battle where the ships were pounding the enemy very close by. In the radio traffic between the ship and the Army spotter, Gene heard the call sign *"Pivot Point."* That's right, now Gene was on the receiving end of the help provided by his old ship, the USS Porterfield. Small world.

Gene went on to a 20-year career in the Army, including a short assignment to Vietnam. I sent him a ball cap with "WW-II ... Korea ... Vietnam Veteran" on the front.

But Gene was not finished with life following close to 30 years of service to his country. After retirement, Gene went to college and became a Baptist Pastor. He moved back to his old home state of Minnesota and started a church up toward the Canadian border. In fact, Gene and his wife Gloria started 17 Christian ministries over twenty-five years in that remote part of Minnesota.

The last time I saw Gene was on the sidewalk outside the San Diego airport. I had driven him to the airport after the

2016 reunion and watched as he was wheeled into the airport on his way home.

Gene Beckstrom ... what an honor to have known him.

Adam von Dioszeghy

Lt(jg) Adam von Dioszeghy and I served together on the Porterfield in 1965-66 including one deployment together to the war zone off Vietnam. Mr. von D, as he was known around the ship, made three such deployments.

Adam, as I now call him, was an officer and I was enlisted, so it couldn't be said we were friends – comrades and shipmates, but not friends.

Adam was a memorable fellow, and I retained fond, but faint, memories of him over the years. He was the Office in Charge (OIC) in a small compartment called IC/Plot. This was the control center from which out five 5" guns were controlled. There was a rack of large switches which controlled the various modes of each gun mount. The centerpiece of this space was the MK-1A fire control computer, an electro/mechanical monster full of gears and other sundry mechanical and electrical things and many dials and knobs on the top. No one knew how it worked, and fortunately it never broke. There were several operators twirling those knobs according to directions given to the ship from on-shore spotters. One position was for range, another for bearing, and a third, which I manned, for elevation.

Mr. von D was the OIC and also the officer who actually pulled the gun triggers on a gyro unit just to the left of my station, so at General Quarters we stood shoulder to shoulder.

As I said, Mr. von D was memorable. He was always trying to liven things up and lift the spirits of the rest of us with small talk, silly jokes and the like. He talked with an accent and had a strange sounding name beginning with van or von. For years I thought he was Dutch.

We went our separate ways for 50+ years, but in recent years at a ship reunion in Denver I finally got a copy of the cruise book for the ships West Pac cruise of 1966. In looking through the roster I came across the name von Dioszeghy. Curiosity got the best of me and I did an internet search for that name. I found the Facebook page of an Aliz von Dioszeghy, a lady. I emailed Aliz describing myself and that crazy Dutchman Adam, and our experiences together back in the 1960s.

Bingo ... Adam responded promptly and thus began an unlikely friendship as we corresponded back and forth, and I finally tracked him down. Then in May 2017 Diana and I visited Adam & Aliz in Hungary.

It turns out that Adam had written his life story. And what an amazing story it is – 440 pages.

Adam was a World War II veteran at the tender age of 7 when he and his mother survived the war raging directly at their door step in Budapest as the Soviet Red Army was pushing the occupying German army out of Hungary.

Following the war, Adam and his mother suffered for years under a brutal communist regime. Adam and his mother were of the aristocracy; he a Baron and his mother a Baroness. His grandfather was a member of parliament and sat in that magnificent parliament building you often see on the Viking River Cruise TV adds. But a heritage of privilege was lost as the communist leadership made life brutally uncomfortable for Adam and his mother.

As a late teen ager, Adam entered university in hopes of becoming an engineer. That was late 1956, the year that revolution broke out in Hungary. It started with the students, but quickly virtually all segments of Hungarian society rebelled against the communist masters; students, factory workers, police, military, farmers and even segments of local government rose up in rebellion. The Soviet masters evacuated the army from Budapest but replaced them with Russian troops and tanks from the interior of Russia and savagely crushed the revolution. Adam was twice wounded, and in the dead of night he and his mother, along with tens of thousands of others, escaped to Austria.

Adam eventually made his way to Menlo Park California where he learned English, became a US citizen and earned a degree from Stanford University.

As the Vietnam War was building up, Adam joined the US Navy and served his new nation with gratitude.

Following his Navy service, Adam went back to Stanford and earned a Law degree and practiced law in Northern California for 35 years. He met Aliz, the love of his life, in California and they married.

They retired in 2000. Were they finished with adventure by then? No ... they moved to Hungary where they began a new life and have lived there since retirement.

So that's the Readers Digest short version of the life and times of Adam & Aliz von Dioszeghy. I have written extensively about them on my blog AYearningForPublius.Wordpress.com. Under CATEGORIES, click on "von Dioszeghy" to read more.

Adam and Aliz have authored three books which can be found on Amazon. I highly recommend them.

Bridging Two Worlds The story of Adam; in Hungary, in America as a refugee, as a Naval officer, as a lawyer and return to Hungary.
Postcards from Pannonia A new life for Adam and Aliz in the Hungarian countryside.

The Bridge Re-Crossed A collection of autobiographical vignettes, with a thematic emphasis on the author returning to the country of his birth after a 45-year absence in the U.S.

I have also written a book Budapest at War: The Story of Hungarian Freedom Fighter Adam von Dioszeghy. Available on Amazon.

Additionally, I have included Adam's story in a book Yearning for Liberty, also available on Amazon.

Yes indeed! I would say a return to "Pivot Point" has been large in my life.

Some Final Tributes

The 1'st USS Laffey (DD-459)

These next few words are here with the permission of John Dough. John's father was a survivor of the 1'st USS Laffey when it was sunk in 1942 off the coast of Guadalcanal. John's son Cole is also a 'destroyer man' and I hope this story brings a tear to your eye and a bit of a puffed-up chest.

These pictures were taken off the coast of Guadalcanal, where Cole's grandfather's destroyer (DD-459) was sunk in battle in 1942. The Captain of the ship Cole is on changed course to sail there so they could pay their respects to the sailors that went down that early morning. While they were floating above the shipwreck over a thousand feet down, Cole dropped a wreath in the water as a memorial. The wreath was a weighted sailors hat with a handmade brass plaque. Cole then had his re-enlistment ceremony topside, above the shipwreck. He is pictured with the Chief Petty Officer taking the oath to defend our country again. As a father I cannot put it into words the amount of pride that I have for such a brave young man. Fair wind and calm seas till your return my son........

A tribute to Cole's grandfather's shipmates

Cole's grandfather

Reenlisting at "Iron Bottom Sound."

The 2'nd USS Laffey (DD-724)

Please read a more complete history of this great ship than I am able to provide here by going to the following web site. And stand by to hold your breath in amazement at the record of this ship and its crew:
http://en.wikipedia.org/wiki/USS_Laffey_(DD-724)#World War Il

In summary, Laffey, "The Ship That Would Not Die" supported the D-Day invasion at Normandy; then she steamed literally to the other side of the world and participated in the South Pacific island battles and the liberation of the Philippines via the naval actions at Leyte Gulf.

During operations north of Okinawa, Laffey came under intense Kamikaze attack from some 50 Japanese suicide bombers ... and she survived to fight another day.

Laffey was not finished as WW-II came to an end. Following decommissioning she was again recommissioned and participated in the Korean War, and in various operations during the Cold War.

Laffey received the US Presidential Unit Citation and five battle stars for World War Il service, the Korean Presidential Unit Citation and two battle stars for Korean War service, and the Meritorious Unit Commendation.

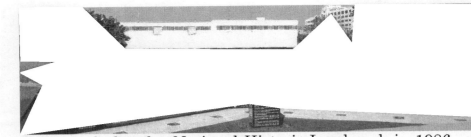

Laffey was declared a National Historic Landmark in 1986 and currently resides in Charleston, South Carolina as a museum ship.

Battle of Leyte Gulf Memorial - Taffy 3
San Diego, California

The Battle of Samar was the centermost action of the Battle of Leyte Gulf, one of the largest naval battles in history, which took place in the Philippine Sea off Samar Island, in the Philippines on October 25, 1944. As the only major action in the larger battle where the Americans were largely unprepared against the opposing forces, it has been cited by historians as one of the greatest military mismatches in naval history.

> "In no engagement of its entire history has the United States Navy shown more gallantry, guts and gumption than in those two morning hours between 0730 and 0930 off Samar "—Samuel Eliot Morison, History of United States Naval
> Operations in World Warn, Volume Xll, Leyte

A Japanese surface force of 4 battleships, 2 cruisers, and 11 destroyers battered earlier in the larger battle and thought to have been in retreat, instead turned around unobserved and stumbled upon the northernmost of the three groups, Task Unit 77.4.3 ("Taffy 3"), commanded by Rear Admiral Clifton Sprague. Taffy 3's few destroyers and slower destroyer escorts possessed neither the firepower nor armor to effectively oppose the Japanese force, but nevertheless desperately attacked with 5"/38 caliber guns and torpedoes to cover the retreat of their slow "jeep" carriers. Aircraft from the carriers of Taffy 1, 2, and 3, including FM-2 Wildcats, F6F Hellcats and TBM Avengers, strafed, bombed, torpedoed, rocketed, depth-charged, fired at least one .38 caliber handgun and made numerous "dry" runs at the attacking force when they ran out of ammunition.

Letter from an airline pilot: He writes:

My lead flight attendant came to me and said, "We have an H.R. On this flight." (H.R. Stands for human remains.) "Are they military?" I asked.

'Yes', she said.

'Is there an escort?' I asked.

'Yes, I've already assigned him a seat'.

'Would you please tell him to come to the flight deck. You can board him early," I said.

A short while later, a young army sergeant entered the flight deck. He was the image of the perfectly dressed soldier. He introduced himself and I asked him about his soldier. The escorts of these fallen soldiers talk about them as if they are still alive and still with us.

'My soldier is on his way back to Virginia,' he said. He proceeded to answer my questions but offered no words.

I asked him if there was anything I could do for him and he said no. I told him that he had the toughest job in the military and that I appreciated the work that he does for the families of our fallen soldiers. The first officer and I got up out of our seats to shake his hand. He left the flight deck to find his seat.

We completed our pre-flight checks, pushed back and performed an uneventful departure. About 30 minutes into our flight I received a call from the lead flight attendant in the cabin. 'I just found out the family of the soldier we are carrying, is on board', she said. She then proceeded to tell me that the father, mother, wife and 2-year old daughter were escorting their son, husband, and father home. The family was upset because they were unable to see the container that the soldier was in before we left. We were on our way to a major hub at which the family was going to wait four hours for the connecting flight home to Virginia.

The father of the soldier told the flight attendant that knowing his son was below him in the cargo compartment and being unable to see him was too much for him and the family to bear. He had asked the flight attendant if there was anything that could be done to allow them to see him upon our arrival. The family wanted to be outside by the cargo door to watch the soldier being taken off the airplane. I could hear the desperation in the flight attendants voice when she asked me if there was anything I could do. 'I'm on it', I said. I told her that I would get back to her.

Airborne communication with my company normally occurs in the form of e-mail like messages. I decided to bypass this system and contact my flight dispatcher directly on a secondary radio. There is a radio operator in the operations control center who connects you to the telephone of the dispatcher. I was in direct contact with the dispatcher. I explained the situation I had on board with the family and what it was the family wanted. He said he understood and that he would get back to me.

Two hours went by and I had not heard from the dispatcher. We were going to get busy soon and I needed to know what to tell the family. I sent a text message asking for an update. I
Saved the return message from the dispatcher and the following is the text:

> 'Captain, sorry it has taken so long to get back to you. There is policy on this now and I had to check on a few things. Upon your arrival a dedicated escort team will meet the aircraft.
>
> The team will escort the family to the ramp and plane side. A van will be used to load the remains with a secondary van for the family. The family will be taken to their departure area and escorted into the terminal where the remains can be seen on the ramp. It is a private area for the family only. When the connecting aircraft arrives, the family will be escorted onto the ramp and plane side to watch the remains being loaded for the final leg home. Captain, most of us here in flight control are veterans. Please pass our condolences on to the family. Thanks.'

I sent a message back telling flight control thanks for a good job. I printed out the message and gave it to the lead flight attendant to pass on to the father. The lead flight attendant was very thankful and told me, 'You have no idea how much this will mean to them.'

Things started getting busy for the descent, approach and landing. After landing, we cleared the runway and taxied to the ramp area. The ramp is huge with 15 gates on either side of the alleyway. It is always a busy area with aircraft maneuvering every which way to enter and exit. When we entered the ramp and checked in with the ramp controller, we were told

That all traffic was being held for us.

There is a team in place to meet the aircraft, we were told. It looked like it was all coming together, then I realized that once we turned the seat belt sign off, everyone would stand up at once and delay the family from getting off the airplane. As we approached our gate, I asked the co-pilot to tell the ramp controller we were going to stop short of the gate to make an announcement to the passengers. He did that and the ramp controller said, 'Take your time.'

I stopped the aircraft and set the parking brake. I pushed the public address button and said, 'Ladies and gentleman, this is your Captain speaking I have stopped short of our gate to make a special announcement. We have a passenger on board who deserves our honor and respect. His Name is Private -----, a soldier who recently lost his life. Private ----- is under your feet in the cargo hold. Escorting him today is Army
Sergeant -----. Also, on board are his father, mother, wife, and daughter. Your entire flight crew is asking for all passengers to remain in their seats to allow the family to exit the aircraft first. Thank you.'

We continued the turn to the gate, came to a stop and started our shutdown procedures. A couple of minutes later I opened the cockpit door. I found the two forward flight attendants crying, something you just do not see. I was told that after we came to a stop, every passenger on the aircraft stayed in their seats, waiting for the family to exit the aircraft.

When the family got up and gathered their things, a passenger slowly started to clap his hands. Moments later more passengers joined in and soon the entire aircraft was clapping. Words of 'God Bless You', 'I'm sorry', 'thank you', 'be proud', and other kind words were uttered to the family as they made their way down the aisle and out of the airplane.

They were escorted down to the ramp to finally be with their loved one.

Many of the passengers disembarking thanked me for the announcement I had made. They were just words, I told them, I could say them over and over again, but nothing I say will bring back that brave soldier.

I respectfully ask that all of you reflect on this event and the sacrifices that millions of our men and women have made to ensure our freedom and safety in these USA, Canada, Australia New Zealand, England.

Foot note:

I know everyone who has served their country who reads this will have tears in their eyes, including me.

Please send this on after a short prayer for our service men and women.

They die for me and mine and you and yours and deserve our honor and respect.

'Lord, hold our troops in your loving hands. protect them as they protect us. Bless them and their families for the selfless acts they perform for us in our time of need. In Jesus Name, Amen. '

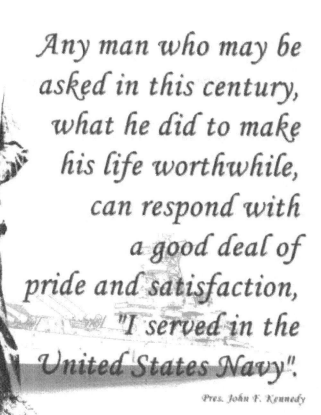

Any man who may be asked in this century, what he did to make his life worthwhile, can respond with a good deal of pride and satisfaction, "I served in the United States Navy".

Pres. John F. Kennedy

Recommended reading and browsing:

- The Last Stand of the Tin Can Sailor: The Extraordinary World War Il Story of the U S. Navy's Finest Hour - by James D. Hornfisher
- Sea of Thunder: Four Commanders and the Last Great Naval Campaign 1941-1945 - by Evan Thomas
- Down to the Sea: An Epic Story of Naval Disaster and Heroism in World War Il - by Bruce Henderson
- Halsey's Typhoon: The True Story of a Fighting Admiral, an Epic Storm, and an Untold Rescue - by Bob Drury
- Destroyers: Greyhounds of the Sea https://www.facebook.com/groups/DDGreyhounds/
- The National Association of Destroyer Veterans
- http://destroyers.org/
- USS Porterfield DD-682/USS Balch DD-363 https://www.facebook.com/groups/75302072915/
- http://en.wikipedia.org/wiki/USS_Porterfield_(DD-682) http://en.wikipedia.org/wiki/USS_Balch_(DD-363)
- Destroyers History http://www.destroyerhistory.org/
- Naval Historical Center http://www.history.navy.mil/
- Help Save our Historic US Navy Destroyers - A great video http://www.youtube.com/watch?v=A_BxKrR7Kl4
- A Yearning for Publius: the authors' blog http://ayearningforpublius.wordpress.com/
- (Under "Categories", click on Navy)
- The following are web sites and videos from which I have borrowed clips for my own video and this book:

- The Lucky Few, The story of the USS Kirk
  http://www.youtube.com/watch?v=S9svL4j9xCc
- USS Kirk Association web site
  http://www.kirk1087.Org/
- Hero Ships Full Episode 8: USS Laffey
  https://www.youtube.com/watch?v=DvIr4mWNt0c
- Quest for Sunken Warships: USS Murphy
  https://www.bing.com/videos/search?q=%e2%80%a2+Quest+for+Sunken+Warships%3a+USS+Murphy&view=detail&mid=C7A8EF4BDB14F28D3D79C7A8EF4BDB14F28D3D79&FORM=VIRE
- Discovery & History
  http://www.ussmurphydd603.com/Movies.html
- Discovery of the USS Murphy (DD-603) and recreation of the collision
  https://youtu.be/TDqooIGZ1BA
- USS Murphy DD-603 Association web site
  http://www.ussmurphydd603.com/
- Destroyer Crew Life: Destroyer men 1970 US Navy
  https://www.youtube.com/watch?v=kr4_RC4oZ4s

Museum Ships

The following are US Navy Destroyer (DD) and Destroyer Escort (DE) historical museum ships. There are other museum ships around the country of many types, and I encourage you to visit them. You can find them at the "Historic Naval Ships Association " at their web site http://www.hnsa.org/

USS Barry DD-933 - Washington, DC
USS Casin Young DD-793 - Boston, Massachusetts
USS Edson DD-946 - Bay City, Michigan
USS Joseph P. Kennedy - Fall River, Massachusetts
   + Battleship USS Massachusetts (BB-59)
   _+USS Lionfish (SS-298) + VI' boat and more
USS Kidd DD-661 -- Baton Rouge, Louisiana
USS Laffey DD-724 -- Charleston, South Carolina
USS Slater DE-766 -- Albany, New York

USS Stewart DE-238 -- Galveston, Texas

USS The Sullivans DD-537 - Buffalo, New York USS Turner Joy DD-951 - Bremerton Washington

Other excellent museum ships:
USS Arizona (BB-39)   Pearl Harbor, Hawaii
USS Missouri (BB-63)   Pearl Harbor, Hawaii
USS Bowfin (SS-287)   Pearl Harbor, Hawaii
USS Midway (CV-41)   San Diego, California USS Intrepid (CV-11)   New York City

We have no government armed with power capable of contending with human passions unbridled by morality and religion. Avarice, ambition, revenge or gallantry would break the strongest cords of our Constitution as a whale goes through a net. Our Constitution is designed only for a moral and religious people. It is wholly inadequate for any other.

John Adams (1735 - 1826)

It is not the critic who counts; not the man who points out how the strong man stumbles, or where the doer of deeds could have done them better. The credit belongs to the man who is actually in the arena, whose face is marred by dust and sweat and blood; who strives valiantly; who errs, who comes short again and again, because there is no effort without error and shortcoming; but who does actually strive to do the deeds; who knows great enthusiasms, the great devotions; who spends himself in a worthy cause; who at the best knows in the end the triumph of high achievement, and who at the worst, if he fails, at least fails while daring greatly, so that his place shall never be with those cold and timid souls who neither know victory nor defeat.

Theodore Roosevelt

For in this modern world, the instruments of warfare are not solely for waging war. Far more importantly, they are the means for controlling peace. Naval officers must therefore understand not only how to fight a war, but how to use the tremendous power which they operate to sustain a world of liberty and justice, without unleashing the powerful instruments of destruction and chaos that they have at their command."

Admiral Arleigh Burke, CNO, 1 August 1961

HOW TO SIMULATE BEING A SAILOR

1. Buy a steel dumpster, paint it gray inside and out, and live in it for six months.
2. Run all the pipes and wires in your house exposed on the walls.
3. Repaint your entire house every month.
4. Renovate your bathroom. Build a wall across the middle of the bathtub and move the shower head to chest level. When you take showers, make sure you turn off the water while you soap down.
5. Put lube oil in your humidifier and set it on high.
6. Once a week, blow compressed air up your chimney, making sure the wind carries the soot onto your neighbor's house. Ignore his complaints.
7. Once a month, take all major appliances apart and then reassemble them.
8. Raise the thresholds and lower the headers of your front and back door so that you either trip or bang your head every time you pass through them.
9. Disassemble and inspect your lawnmower every week.
10. On Mondays, Wednesdays, and Fridays, turn your water heater temperature up to 200 degrees. On Tuesdays and Thursdays, turn the water heater off. On Saturdays and Sundays tell your family they use too much water during the week, so no bathing will be allowed.
11. Raise your bed to within 6" of the ceiling, so you can't turn over without getting out and then getting back in.
12. Sleep on the shelf in your closet. Replace the closet door with a curtain. Have your spouse whip open the

curtain about 3 hours after you go to sleep, shine a flashlight in your eyes, and say "Sorry, wrong rack."
13. Make your family qualify to operate each appliance in your house - dishwasher operator, blender technician, etc.
14. Have your neighbor come over each day at 0500, blow a whistle so loud Helen Keller could hear it, and shout "Reveille, reveille, all hands heave out and trice up."
15. Have your mother-in-law write down everything she's going to do the following day, then have her make you stand in your back yard at 0600 while she reads it to you.
16. Submit a request chit to your father-in-law requesting permission to leave your house before 1500.
17. Empty all the garbage bins in your house and sweep the driveway three times a day, whether it needs it or not.
18. Have your neighbor collect all your mail for a month, read your magazines, and randomly lose every 5th item before delivering it to you.
19. Watch no TV except for movies played in the middle of the night. Have your family vote on which movie to watch, then show a different one.
20. When your children are in bed, run into their room with a megaphone shouting that your home is under attack and ordering them to their battle stations. (Now general quarters, general quarters, all hands man your battle stations.)
21. Make your family menu a week ahead of time without consulting the pantry or refrigerator.
22. Post a menu on the kitchen door informing your family that they are having steak for dinner. Then make them wait in line for an hour. When they finally get to the kitchen, tell them you are out of steak, but they can have dried ham or hot dogs. Repeat daily until they ignore the menu and just ask for hot dogs.

23. Bake a cake. Prop up one side of the pan so the cake bakes unevenly.
24. Spread icing real thick to level it off.
25. Get up every night around midnight and have a peanut butter and jelly sandwich on stale bread. (mid-rats)
26. Set your alarm clock to go off at random during the night. At the alarm, jump up and dress as fast as you can, making sure to button your top shirt button and tuck your pants into your socks. Run out into the backyard and uncoil the garden hose.
27. Every week or so, throw your cat or dog in the pool and shout "Man overboard port side!" Rate your family members on how fast they respond.
28. Put the headphones from your stereo on your head, but don't plug them in. Hang a paper cup around your neck on a string. Stand in front of the stove and speak into the paper cup "Stove manned and ready." After an hour or so, speak into the cup again "Stove secured." Roll up the headphones and paper cup and stow them in a shoebox.
29. Place a podium at the end of your driveway. Have your family stand watches at the podium, rotating at 4-hour intervals. This is best done when the weather is worst. January is a good time.
30. When there is a thunderstorm in your area, get a wobbly rocking chair, sit in it and rock as hard as you can until you become nauseous. Make sure to have a supply of stale crackers in your shirt pocket.
31. For former engineers: bring your lawn mower into the living room and run it all day long.
32. Make coffee using eighteen scoops of budget priced coffee grounds per pot and allow the pot to simmer for 5 hours before drinking.
33. Have someone under the age of ten give you a haircut with sheep shears.

34. Sew the back pockets of your jeans on the front.
35. Lock yourself and your family in the house for six weeks. Tell them that at the end of the 6th week you are going to take them to Disney World for "liberty. At the end of the 6th week, inform them the trip to Disney World has been canceled because they need to get ready for an inspection, and it will be another week before they can leave the house.
36. If you were a radioman take brown paper bags, fill with newspapers and staple them closed. Pile them in the corner of your room and sleep on them because its more comfortable then your rack and the radio room has A/C.
37. Refuel your car from the tanker truck on the freeway at 60 miles/hour.

The places we lived

In a gun mount

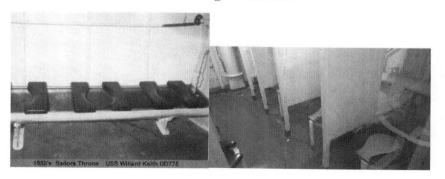

The not so private head.

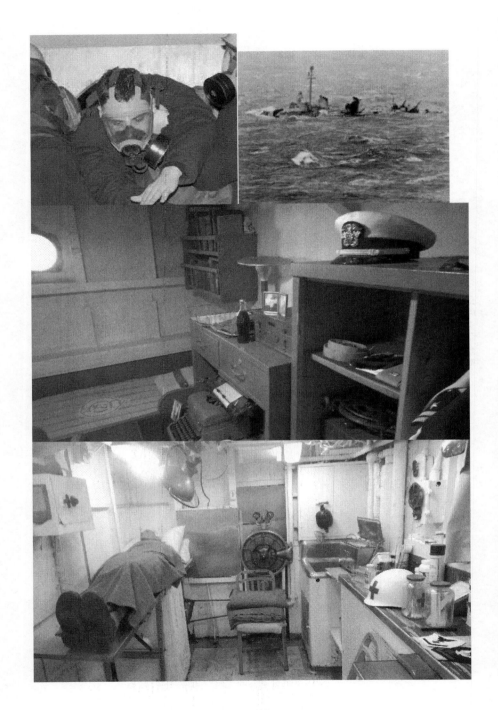

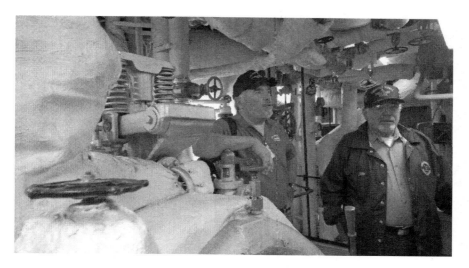

And sometimes a rough neighborhood.

Heritage

About the author

d in Butte, Montana and joined the Navy in 1964 at 20 years of age. Following his years of active duty, including a tour to the Vietnam war zone in 1966, he finished college with a degree in mathematics from San Diego State University and entered the field of software development.

Don's connection with the Navy did not end at the completion of his enlistment. For many years after his destroyer assignments he was a software developer at Cubic Defense Systems, slinging code for the US Navy & Air Force Tactical Aircrew Combat Training System (TACTS/ACMI), also known as the Top Gun system, the premier online training system for US and allied combat aircrews.

Don has a lifelong interest in history, politics and current events which is reflected in his writings. In recent years, Don has experienced a rekindling of interest in his Navy service and has reconnected with shipmates from his old ship by joining the USS Balch/Porterfield Reunion Association.

Don blogs at www.ayearningforpublius.wordpress.com, writing about politics, faith, culture, science and more ... things that should never be talked about in polite company.

Don's books can be found at:
www.amazon.com/author/donjohnsonbooks
http://www.blurb.com/user/donanddiana

Some reader remarks on this book

This is from a note I received from **Eula Rotter**, the widow of a WW-II sailor, and one of those left behind in 1943. We met Eula last year at our first USS Balch-Porterfield reunion, and again was with her at this years reunion in Buffalo (the 39'th annual reunion of those two ships).

I presented complementary copies of the book to all 22 sailors present as well as 3 widow - Eula was one of those. Here is her note:

Good morning from Carson City,

I just finished reading your book. Super good reading - a "tear jerker" in some places, but a true book of Navy experiences.

Thank you so much.

Nice meeting and talking to you, Diana.

Till we meet again -

Eula

From *Carolyn Gunnon:* This friend of mine is amazing! Not only does his book provide its readers with true to life facts, stories, and photos, it also includes Don's well chosen, pertinent messages from The Great Book...just another reason to get it and share in his pride and devotion to his country!

Hi Don, *Carolyn Gunnon* gave me your book 'I Didn't Want to Worry You Mom' and I really enjoyed it. Thanks for putting all the history together in this book.

I was in the Navy from 4/1/1958 to 6/15/1962. My 1st ship was the USS Borie, DD-704. Our main claim to fame was retrieving the 1st monkey sent into space in 1959. Shortly thereafter I was given orders to go to new construction for the 1st Destroyer Guided Missile Destroyer, Charles F Adams, DDG-2. It was the first DDG to built from the keel on up. It was a show ship (it was said that F in the name stood for field day). We took it to Europe impress our allies.

There is an ongoing effort to move the ADAMS to a naval museum in Jacksonville FL.

Bud Meyer

Recently Diana and I attended our second reunion of the two ships USS Balch and USS Porterfield:

https://ayearningforpublius.wordpress.com/2013/09/15/stepping-into-a-history-book-a-us-navy-destroyer-reunion/

In Buffalo were 4 "tin can" sailor veterans from WW II and 18 others who served after WW-II through Korea, Vietnam and through the Cold War until the ship was decommissioned in 1969. You can read some of what took place in Buffalo at:

https://ayearningforpublius.wordpress.com/2014/09/19/kick-off-event-for-the-book-i-didnt-want-to-worry-you-mom/

I showed the introductory video, and followed that with a presentation of complementary copies of the book to the 22 sailors as well as three widows in attendance.

One thing I found interesting was that we had 22 sailors in attendance but about twice that many others - family and friends, sons and daughters, brothers and sisters. So the reunion was not just a bunch of us old timers telling the same old stale stories once more ... no - this was a family affair and an affair that had a lot of love and honoring and respect shown.

This being my first attempt at creating a book, I really had no feel for how good or bad it might be ... I thought it was good of course, and was pleased with it - but had I created a dud?

But after the video and book presentation I received many sincere complements and comments from sailors and family alike.

Sam Thomas, a 91-year-old veteran of both the Balch and Porterfield, approached me afterwards, shook my hand and told me that portions of the video brought tears to his eyes ... and no it was not the bang and boom segments, but those that showed the humanity of the sailors.

Gene Beckstrom, 89 years old and a 6-year Navy veteran and shipmate of the Porterfield from 1943-1946 followed that with a 20 year Army career which included 5 major battles in Korea as an infantryman. After Gene's military career, he entered the ministry and in the past 25 years founded and established 19 churches in the northern remote reaches of Minnesota.

Gene told me that portions of the book brought tears to his eyes.

Again, these comments served as validation of the book, its motivations and its contents.

From Gene Beckstrom,

This month has been one of the highlights of my life. My son Bruce drove me to Buffalo, New York, for a reunion of the USS Porterfield (DD-682), the ship I served on and put into commission ("Plank Owner", Navy persons would know what that means).

I was just 16 years old and knew that I was the smartest person that walked the earth.

("Boot Camp") changed that attitude and I found out that I was the "dumbest" person on this earth. From Boot Camp I was sent to San Pedro, California and was assigned to the USS Porterfield. Upon arrival I found a dry dock and a big hunk of steel sitting on some wood wedges. This was my introduction to the ship I would serve on from commissioning to de-commissioning (1943-1945). Many new experiences I was to have and MANY lessons to be learned the "Hard Way."

Learning to take orders and not asking "WHY" was the hardest for me as I had not completely learned this lesson yet, and I found out that there were many who would teach me this lesson the hard way, and it was for my and other shipmates welfare because lives will be at risk. The last lesson I learned before we set sail for the South Pacific was that if you don't return to the ship from weekend liberty there are consequences. I failed to return and was taken to the "Treasure Island Brig" and was confined until several days before we departed for the South Pacific. I was also confined to the ship (no shore liberty) so it would be months before I was able to put my feet on solid ground (another lesson learned the hard way).

The next two years many lessons were learned the hard way and this young sailor became a man and proud of the USS Porterfield and the men that served on her. Many of my shipmates that had a "top side" battle station received numerous wounds and some never made it back. The one battle that stands out is the Leyte operation, close and up front with the whole Japanese Naval fleet. A Japanese surface force of 4 battleships, 2 cruiser, and 11 destroyers.

I am indebted to a shipmate and brother in Christ, Don Johnson and his wife Diana for the friendship we have since meeting at the Salt Lake City reunion last year. Don has complied a book, "I Didn't Want to Worry You Mom; ... (But sometimes it got a little scary and dangerous out there!) This book contains the majority of the Naval battles through WW II and Vietnam and the first-hand interviews with some of the survivors. If you are interested in naval history, I recommend you purchase this book and you will be surprised of its contents of factual naval history.

Pastor Gene - Northern Minnesota Ministries

Swan Lake; Road Baptist Church--Floodwood Baptist Chapel

This from **Commander Hugh Doyle** - Engineering Officer of the USS Kirk (DE-1087) during Operation Frequent Wind as shown in the book, and featured on my video.

Captain Paul Jacobs, please meet Don Johnson, a fellow "Tin Can Sailor" who was an active duty Fire Control Technician in USS PORTERFIELD (DD-682) in Westpac from 1966 to 1968, and later served as a reservist in USS SHIELDS (DD-596). Don is now retired and living in New Haven, CT. He is the author of a great book "I Didn't Want to Worry You Mom... (...But sometimes it got a little scary and dangerous out there!)"

Don's book is an outstanding collection of his own personal stories (including a collision at sea in SHIELDS), and many other tales he has gathered from other "Tin Can Sailors" that honor and illustrate the life of "Destroyer Men" down through our history. Our USS KIRK connection to Don is that he chose the story of our good ship KIRK's role in Operation Frequent Wind to be included in his book. Using our documentary "The Lucky Few" as his source, Don faithfully tells our story (spanning 15 pages of his nearly 140-page work.)

Captain, I have met Don personally, and he is a fine man. I told him a lot of the "back story" to our KIRK role in Frequent Wind, and I shared with him a few of my own personal "sea stories" about our Captain (don't worry -- just the "good" ones!).

Don Johnson, please meet Captain Paul Jacobs. I served under this good man for half my tour in USS KIRK, and I survived. And that's not a joke -- I was a "Marketing" major at Villanova University, and when the Navy discovered that I was a business graduate, they quite naturally decided to make me a steam engineer. When I discovered that our new Captain was in fact a professional Marine Engineer graduate of Maine Maritime Academy, I was shaking in my boots. I thought "Jake" would see me an "engineer-pretender" and my budding Navy career would come to a screeching halt. Turns out, he was very forgiving (thank God!), and I could not have asked for a better "boss." Jake was the right man at the right time in the right place when Vietnam fell, and the best Captain I had in my 20 years in the Navy.

So, Don meet Jake; Jake meet Don.

All the best,

Hugh

I got word recently that a 90-year-old sailor and veteran of the South Pacific sea battles was to take an Honor Flight trip with his son to the memorials in Washington DC. We were asked to send cards and letters and other mementos to him, so he could have a mail bag when he returned. I sent a copy of my book. I never knew **Len Lohne,** even though he was raised and spent the majority of his 90 years in the same church Diana and I have been attending the past 5+ years, so we did have some overlap there.

When Len returned from the Honor Flight event, and the day after we returned from our ship reunion, Len called me and thanked me profusely for compiling the book and sending him a copy. He told me that he read it cover to cover in one sitting and enjoyed it very much. His wife told me that she also was looking forward to reading it. We also talked a bit about his Navy experience, and about his life following the war. A very delightful man, and one I wish I had met and known during the time we shared at church.

Len's comments about the book served as additional validation to me as to my motivations for the book and in choosing the contents.

The book is intended to honor those who served, as well as those who were left behind not knowing what was happening to their loved ones, and not even knowing if they would return.

Thanks so much for reading!

Now if I could ask a favor of you? Would you be so kind as to write a review of this book at the Amazon site?

amazon.com/author/donjohnsonbooks

Thanks again.

Made in the USA
Middletown, DE
03 September 2018